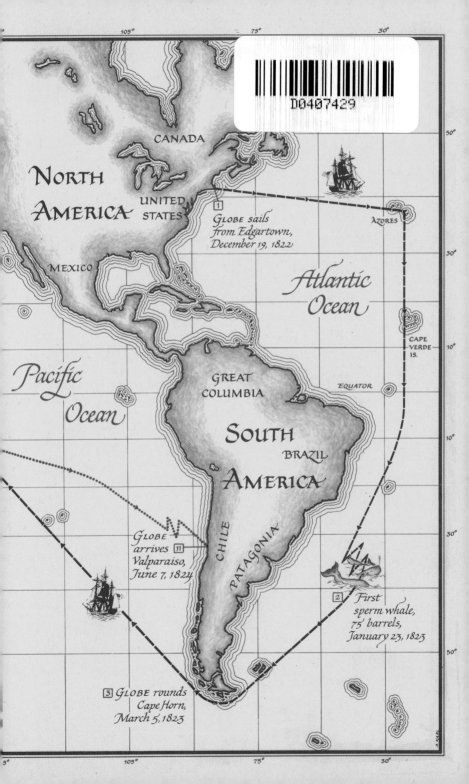

NORTH AMERICA

CANADA

UNITED STATES

MEXICO

Pacific Ocean

AZORES

Atlantic Ocean

CAPE VERDE IS.

EQUATOR

GREAT COLUMBIA

SOUTH AMERICA

BRAZIL

CHILE

PATAGONIA

1 *Globe sails from Edgartown, December 19, 1822*

11 *Globe arrives Valparaiso, June 7, 1824*

2 *First sperm whale, 75 barrels, January 23, 1823*

3 *Globe rounds Cape Horn, March 5, 1823*

105°   75°   30°

50°

30°

10°

10°

30°

50°

5°   105°   75°   30°

May 77

The Mutiny on the Globe

Edwin P. Hoyt

MUTINY ON THE GLOBE

Random House   New York

Copyright © 1975 by Edwin P. Hoyt

All rights reserved under International and Pan-American Copyright Con-
ventions. Published in the United States by Random House, Inc., New York,
and simultaneously in Canada by Random House of Canada Limited,
Toronto.

Library of Congress Cataloging in Publication Data

Hoyt, Edwin Palmer.
The mutiny on the Globe.

Bibliography: p.
1. Globe Mutiny, 1824. 2. Globe (Whaling ship)
I. Title.
DU710.H69 1975   910'.453   75-5779
ISBN 0-394-49365-6

Manufactured in the United States of America

9 8 7 6 5 4 3 2

First Edition

*To Edouard Stackpole, the world's greatest
expert on whaling and whalers*

THE STORY of the mutiny aboard the whaler *Globe* is a true story, and it is re-created here from documents and accounts of the mutiny written by survivors and witnesses. It is unusual to be able to reconstruct an event that occurred far out at sea in the year 1824; the reason so much detail exists is that two of the chief mutineer's brothers left accounts of the man and the events, and several other accounts of the voyage and the search for survivors were written in the next few years. The conversations in the book are as related by those survivors and witnesses, as they recalled them.

CONTENTS

THE
VOYAGE

1

THE SAILING

THE SHIP *Globe* out of Nantucket lay fretfully alongside the wharf of Old Town on the island of Martha's Vineyard this December afternoon, rising and falling gently with the swell of the tide and the little harbor chop. There was nothing unusual in the *Globe*'s presence here at the beginning of a voyage, for Old Town (now called Edgartown) was, in the year 1822, the principal outfitting port for Nantucket whaling ships, and anyone who took a good look at the *Globe* would know her for what she was, a whaler.

She lay low in the water, having shipped all provisions for a long voyage. Her sails were neat and clean, which indicated that she was just starting out and was not betweentimes. Her hull was black and proud and fresh of paint, which meant she belonged to a successful shipping firm. But these things did not mark her as a whaler. What did mark her was her shape: blunt and fat and built for work; her three stumpy masts and heavy booms, and above all, her boats. For every whaler sported the same type of craft and they were unmistakable. These boats were twenty-five to thirty feet long, slim, tapered and elegant. They looked fast in the water, and they were. They had to be. In the sea, these craft carried half a dozen men to compete for mastery with the great whales—some of the creatures as long as the

3

whaling ship. No boat could ever be built strong enough to withstand the crushing jaws of a great sperm whale or the lash of the whale's flukes, so they were built sleek, and seaworthy for pursuit, and they had a look about them as cunning as the back of a porpoise at play.

Now the *Globe* was ready to sail, waiting for her new captain, Thomas Worth, to come aboard and begin the voyage to the South Seas, where she would, hopefully, search and kill and take on whale oil and come home "greasy," as she had done before.

The *Globe* was a fine stout ship, just seven years old this December day in 1822, which meant in the prime of her life. And she bore an enviable reputation gained in her previous treks across the seas. Her first captain, George W. Gardner, had led her out to find the new "offshore" whaling grounds near Peru. Nantucket and Martha's Vineyard would never forget that contribution to whaling welfare. That first *Globe* voyage had lasted two and a half years, not a long time by whalers' standards, and Captain Gardner had come home with flags and pennants flying, so that before the *Globe* ever pulled into the Straight Wharf at Nantucket, the merchants on their walks knew that she had brought back 1,890 barrels of precious oil. Next time out, in 1818, the *Globe* had won new honors: she was the first Nantucket vessel, and the first whaler ever, for that matter, to bring home a cargo of more than 2,000 barrels of sperm oil. Captain Gardner was the envy of every sailingman in New England. Christopher Mitchell and Company, owners of the *Globe* and a number of other vessels, were so pleased with Gardner that he could write his own ticket.

The owners had discovered early on that whaling men sailed happily if there was an incentive, so the company was started as a cooperative and continued that way. After the last whaling trip the captain got his 1/16th share (or "lay") ; his first mate got a 1/25th; and the lowly cabin boy got a 1/200th of the profits of the voyage. Under Captain Gardner this meant that the boy got the value of ten barrels of oil for his two-and-a-half-years' work. His share was not great, but no one ever expected to get rich sailing before the mast of a whaler. Yet those years before the mast were essential if a man was to progress in the trade. There was no school for whalers but whaling, and after one voyage the cabin boy of the *Globe* would have little but the money to bring home a few trinkets, buy a decent set of clothes and support himself until the next voyage. On the next voyage he would be a seaman, receiving a 1/165th share. Then he could start moving higher up the ladder, as Captain Gardner had done.

It had been planned that Gardner would take the 295-ton ship out to the offshore grounds this winter, and with any luck he would be home in two years, his holds again filled with sperm oil. With a good catch a captain—even a mate—could expect to earn enough money to buy a house, marry and provide well for his wife. Next step up was to obtain a share in a ship, for while the total expenses of the crew and ship came to one half of the profits of a successful venture, the owners would share in the equivalent of $100,000 or more if the catch exceeded 2,000 barrels. If a captain did his job well, he would soon be a wealthy man.

This easiness of climb was one of the secrets of the whaling trade's success in securing crews. Another factor was the ingrown nature of the society on Nantucket and Martha's Vineyard, where every family knew every other and most of them were in some way related: one of the new captain's cousins was a seaman aboard the *Globe;* one of the coopers was related to the owners. There was nothing unusual in this; the *Globe* was a Nantucket ship and whaling was Nantucket's lifeblood, and to a lesser extent the lifeblood of the Vineyard, whence came Captain Worth and many of the crew.

Captain Gardner had been recruiting crew members for months when suddenly, in the autumn, he announced that he was leaving the Mitchell service to take a bigger ship with an owner's interest in the proceeds. On his last voyage he had grown to trust and like his first mate, Thomas Worth, and he recommended that the Mitchell firm appoint Worth to his old post.

That recommendation carried much weight, for the owners could not possibly know all that occurred on a sailing voyage, and they did not wish to know the seamier sides. They were content when Captain Gardner said First Mate Worth could bring a ship home safely with a cargo of oil, and they asked no more than that.

At twenty-nine, Thomas Worth was the oldest man aboard the *Globe.* He had come up the hard way, shipping out as a young boy, standing his watches as an apprentice and then as an able-bodied seaman. He had learned to climb the futtocks and into the tops, to man the lookout station nearly a hundred feet above the deck of the ship, to sing out that magic phrase "Thar she blows!" which was the action call to the whaling crew.

Worth had risked the dangers of the deep countless times in an open boat, and had been towed far from the mother ship by frightened, puffing whales. He had fought with the other seamen and learned the toughening of the sailor's life. He was beaten with a rope's end and learned to respect the orders of his officers. As he moved aft from the forward berths, Worth learned the essentials of ship's discipline. The captain must maintain his rule at all times by whatever means necessary. Worth had learned this while on board vessels that ran short of water or when the salt beef and salt pork went bad and the ship's biscuits moldered. In such parlous days, only the iron discipline of a captain held the ship and crew together—otherwise it would have been every man for himself, the devil take the hindmost, and rebellion would have reared its ugly head. On that last voyage under Captain Gardner, First Mate Worth had been the chief disciplinarian of the ship. He had knocked men down for disobeying orders and carried the men bodily to the captain if further discipline was needed.

After returning from two very successful trips, Worth had decided to get married on the strength of his shares in the voyages and his hopes for the future. Captain Gardner, a Nantucket man, had detailed Worth to sail the *Globe,* empty, down to Old Town for fitting. Then Worth turned the vessel over to

Second Mate William Beetle, bought a house and got married, then settled down to enjoy a short period of family life before sailing day.

Beetle was another Vineyard man, an intense, large young fellow, three years younger than First Mate Worth. Now on his shoulders fell the weight of discipline.

Discipline?

The deepwater sailors who carried cargoes across the oceans said the whalers did not know what discipline meant. This observation was based on what they saw and heard: slack sails, dirty sides, oil-encrusted booms—and the tales the whaling men told in neutral ports.

What the other sailors said was true of whaling men in one respect: they did not have the same *kind* of discipline as other ships. For example, on a merchant vessel it was four hours on and eight hours off, and men stood regular watches, day in and day out. On a whaler, *everyone* was on watch from dawn to dusk, and then the special "watches" were divided into three, carrying through the night, from dusk till dawn. As a whaler traveled the thousands of miles from Nantucket and Martha's Vineyard to the whaling grounds, there was very little need for the type of discipline so often dispensed with a rope's end on other ships. It was only when the whaler was on station that discipline was taut, and then it was as severe as any in the world, for to a whaling man, discipline was *precision*. In the chase of a whale, immediate response to orders might mean the difference between success and failure, or even life and death. Depending on the nature of the captain, a whaler could be a very happy ship when the men responded to this kind of discipline, and the *Globe* under Captain Gardner *was* a happy ship. The blows occasionally dispensed by Gardner, and more often by First Mate Worth, had been accepted as part of the sailor's lot.

The other disciplinarian aboard the *Globe* was the third mate, but he had very limited authority compared to the captain and the first mate. The third mate was John Lumbert, a Nantucket man, just twenty-five years old. These officers supervised the sailors in the rigging as the sails were raised and lowered, and aided in the general management of the ship.

All the officers lived in the general area called "the cabin," which was located on the second deck and occupied the entire after section of the ship. On the starboard side, aft, the captain had a big stateroom of his own, containing his bed, a tiny desk, sea chest, locker, and racks for stowage of his duffle. Opposite, the three mates were crammed into a similar space. First Mate Worth had a tiny compartment of his own; Second Mate Beetle and Third Mate Lumbert shared one the same size. The remainder of the space aft on this deck was given over to the common cabin where the officers ate, the captain plotted his navigation exercises, and the officers relaxed when there was time. The ship's arms were kept in racks along the bulkhead: cutlasses and pistols and a number of muskets with bayonets, to be used as protection against unfriendly natives on the tropical islands.

For such a small ship as the *Globe,* whose total complement was twenty-one persons, three mates seems an unusually high number, but there was a good reason for it: the tasks of the officers in the processes of whaling. Before Captain Gardner's decision to leave the ship, it was decided that Beetle would be in charge of one of the *Globe*'s three whaleboats; the other two would be commanded by Captain Gardner and Worth. Lumbert would be "boatsteerer" for Captain Gardner, in addition to his general duties.

There were two other harpooner-boatsteerers in the ship, but their position was somewhat different from Lumbert's. These others were officially called boatsteerer, or harpooner. They were not officers, nor were they men before the mast. They lived in the steerage compartment between the forecastle in the bow and the officers' cabin in the stern. They took their meals in the cabin with the officers, but the men did not call them "sir."

In the whaleboat, at the beginning of the chase, the boat-steerer stood in the bow, with his officer at the tiller. At the feet of the boatsteerer were two kegs of neatly coiled line. The officer directed the boat toward the whale, responding to shouts from the boatsteerer, who stood, harpoon in hand, waiting for the proper moment. When he let fly the weapon, the rope began to run out of the kegs. If the thrust was successful, the boat was hooked to whale by harpoon and the long, stretching rope, and the crew was treated to a "Nantucket sleigh ride," a thundering, sizzling trip through the water, perhaps for an hour or so until the sunken whale tired and came to the surface. In the interim it was customary for the harpooner and officer to change stations in the boat, and the officer took up the killing lance while the harpooner steered the boat.

Some of these boatsteerers aspired to be officers, some did not. Their position was envious by the crew's standards, for a boatsteerer received the same lay as the first mate: a 1/25th share of the proceeds of the voyage.

The first boatsteerer was Gilbert Smith; a twenty-year old Vineyard man. Smith was of the ambitious cut; he aspired to become a whaling captain himself. He was a Quaker, very religious, and quiet, slow-going, and conservative in everything he did. He was "old reliable"—a man who could not be expected to show much imagination, but who could be entrusted with any detail and would finish it up in workmanlike style.

The second boatsteerer was a different article altogether. His name was Samuel B. Comstock. He was Nantucket-born and also twenty years old. But that was almost the only point of similarity between the two harpooners. Comstock was blond and handsome, sturdy of frame with bulging muscles, laughing eyes and a strong jaw. He was quick to smile, quick to take offense, quick to fight. That last was not an unusual attribute in a whaling man, but it did make for difficulties on voyages and explained why the stout fists of Captain Gardner and Mate Worth were held in such respect aboard the *Globe*.

Next to the boatsteerers in the steerage lived the two coopers, amid the tools and equipment of their trade. They were lower in rank than the boatsteerers; they ate with the men and went to the galley for their own food like the others before the mast. But they had separate quarters and received a higher share of the profits of the voyage than any seaman. They were the carpenters who kept the ship's woodwork in proper condition, but they also made the barrels that would be needed to store the whale oil.

The first cooper was Rowland Coffin, a young man in his early twenties. He was a nephew of one of the principals in the Mitchell company. Coffin did not aspire to become a captain; after several years at sea he could return to Nantucket to go into the business end of whaling.

Coffin's assistant cooper was Cyrus Hussey, a boy of seventeen, also from Nantucket. He had spent several years in the Mitchell company counting house preparing for a whaling career. It was expected that he would become a whaler, for "Hussey of Nantucket" was a famous whaling name. The family had already given a dozen captains to the sea, and the big frame house in which Cyrus grew up had been built with money from whaling voyages. He was only slightly experienced as a cooper, but an eager, tow-headed young fellow who got on well with officers and men.

The galley of the *Globe* was also located in the steerage, and here John Cleveland, twenty-one years old, held forth. Cleveland was a good enough cook, but he had one failing: he drank to excess. Yet a good ship's cook was not so easy to find that Captain Gardner felt like discharging him. And otherwise Cook Cleveland was perfectly reliable. His position was special, too; he was a member of the crew but the guardian of the food supplies, and in that field a person of authority.

These three, the cook and the two coopers, had one other responsibility. They were the standby "crew" of the ship. If the *Globe* found herself amid a school of whales, all three boats would be launched and this would require the services at the oars of every one of the twelve seamen. Under those conditions, the cook and the two coopers actually sailed the ship. In the absence of all the officers and crew they steered, trimmed the sails and had total responsibility for protecting the vessel and keeping it near the boats.

Up forward, in the forecastle, lived the men before the mast, sleeping in bunks stacked three high in the small compartment, with just enough room in each bunk to squeeze in a straw mattress, blankets and a man. The rest of the fo'c'sle was crowded with their sea chests, bags and gear.

All these seamen were youngsters, not one was halfway through his twenties. The youngest was the cabin boy, Joseph Ignatius Prass, fourteen; being Portuguese-American, he was considered a "foreigner." Next youngest was George Comstock, brother of the boatsteerer; he was just fifteen years old and an apprentice seaman. Columbus Worth, the first mate's nephew, was sixteen and another apprentice; and Rowland Jones, son of a famous Vineyard whaling family, was sixteen and his sidekick.

Then there were the Kidder brothers—Peter, twenty-one, and Stephen, eighteen. They were both able-bodied seamen, "old hands" who had been with Captain Gardner on the last voyage. They came from Martha's Vineyard. So did Nahum Mahurin, an Old Town man in his early twenties.

The remainder of the crew came from places not far away from the two offshore islands. William Lay, seventeen, was from Saybrook, Connecticut. He was a dark-haired young man, much given to reading his Bible and quoting from it. He was a particular friend of young Cyrus Hussey's. Another Saybrook boy was Jeremiah Ingham, who was slightly older than Lay. Then there was Daniel Cook, twenty-two, a mulatto from Boston, one of two men aboard who could never aspire to become whaling captains. The other was Paul Jarret, twenty-four, a Mashpee Indian from Barnstable, Massachusetts. And finally there was Holden Henman from Canton, Massachusetts. That made up the crew of the *Globe*.

With Captain Gardner's announcement that he was leaving the *Globe*, Worth was suddenly catapulted into total responsibility. He chose Beetle to succeed him as first mate, and Lumbert to be second mate. A new man, Nathaniel Fisher, a twenty-year-old Vineyarder, was appointed third mate. The new appointments brought delays, so it was December before the *Globe* was ready to begin her voyage.

On the afternoon of December 14, all crewmen and all officers save the captain were aboard the *Globe*. Since they had left Nantucket for the fitting process in Old Town, they had enjoyed much time ashore. But that was now all ended. The hour of sailing was growing near. The ship's hold was crammed with barrels of provisions, and stacks of oaken staves, and clean, bright iron hoops for barrels. All the knives and spears and harpoons had been checked and replacements made.

Finally, late that afternoon, Captain Worth, the new master, left his bride and his house and came down to the wharf to board the vessel. Everything was ready for a voyage that might last for years.

2

SEEDS OF SORROW

THE MORNING of December 15 dawned bright and cloudless and with a nice onshore breeze, one of those days when the term New England seemed a total misnomer, for the weather was not like England's at all. The *Globe* missed the morning tide; there were too many greenhorns among the young crew to put the loose ends together in time for sailing. So the *Globe* sailed out on the evening tide heading for East Chop, that dangerous ground which a good sailor kept well to port of him as he left the Vineyard.

The sails came up jerkily and awkwardly, but Captain Worth had once been a greenhorn himself and knew from his many voyages that it would take a few days for the crew to shake down and become proficient in the yards.

Not long after sailing, Captain Worth had First Mate Beetle assemble all the crew on the broad deck aft, where he gave them their articles of sailing. He inveighed against liquor, being a stout member of the Society of Friends. The men would have their tot of rum, but there was to be no drunkenness aboard this ship. He alternately threatened and held out the promise of a successful voyage. He told them about the low prices in the slop chest, from which the forgetful and careless would have to draw sea stores that should have been purchased ashore. He promised a twenty-dollar gold piece to the first man to sight a spout, and special rewards for the crew of the first boat that brought in its whale.

Then the men were given their work assignments. They were told the names of their watches and the officers under whom they would serve. In this sense, the boatsteerers were officers of the ship in whaling practice, for each was in charge of a night duty watch. George Comstock and Seamen Ingham, Cook and Mahurin were assigned to Samuel Comstock's waist-boat watch. The other eight men were split between Boatsteerer Smith's larboard boat watch, and Third Mate Fisher's starboard boat watch. The coopers and the cook were the only ones unassigned.

It was the custom on the ship to split up the duty watches as broadly as possible, and three watches did not place too much hardship on any men. During the daylight hours, every man on the ship was on the lookout. Since whale could be found almost anywhere in the waters they would traverse, an officer or a boatsteerer stood at the main masthead in a lookout station, eyes alert, for two hours at a stretch. Similarly, a crewman was always perched high in the foremast topgallant crosstrees; from dawn until dusk that post was manned, the men there also changing station every two hours so a fresh eye could be cast around the horizon.

All this sorting out by the captain and the mates on the rear deck of the *Globe* took less than an hour on sailing day, and then the men moved forward once again to take up their duties.

The ship headed outward, rounding East Chop, and then West Chop, along the route to the open sea, down the channel of Vineyard Sound, a narrow body of water strewn with wrecks and rocks to warn of the dangers that lay along the rugged shores of the Vineyard and the Elizabeth Islands.

The *Globe* was nearly ready to put the pilot ashore on Cuttyhunk Island when every man on deck heard a sharp crack aloft. Gazing upward, Captain Worth saw that the cropjack yard had been carried away. On deck Joseph Prass crossed himself, as befitted his religion, for such ill luck at the outset of a voyage foretold grim tidings about their future. With a curse Beetle ordered the wrecked yard down; men swarmed aloft and cut the lines that held it, and lowered it to the deck before it could foul more important rigging and tear the sails.

Deep into the voyage, the captain might have elected to fix a jury rig and keep on going. But here at the beginning it would have been foolhardy. Worth made his decision swiftly. It was late in the evening, and no time to try to thread their way back through the tortuous passages they had sailed in daylight. Pilot still aboard, the captain headed in to Holmes' Hole, a sheltered little harbor on the north shore of Martha's Vineyard. There he ordered the anchor down, and the ship to stay the night.

The next morning it was back for Old Town, with the men cursing a little at the delay, but the captain grateful that the break had come so close to easy repair stations. The riggers soon had the new cropjack yard secured with shiny tarred rope. But a delay is a delay, and it throws everything out of whack. It was three days before the ship was ready to sail a second time.

One reason was that a Vineyard seaman, Nahum Mahurin, decided to leave. He had convinced himself on the way back from Holmes' Hole that the *Globe* was setting out on an unlucky voyage. Hat in hand, he went to the captain, begging to be released from his contract to make the voyage, and Captain Worth, being a genial person, first tried to convince Mahurin that devils were not streaming along behind the ship's taffrail log, but then he released him. One malcontent could not be allowed to rot the morale of the ship, and it was best to lose him at the beginning of the voyage. Mahurin went off to explain as best he could his reasons for forsaking the ship, and Seaman Constant Lewis shipped in Mahurin's place. Lewis was a nineteen-year-old from the village of Tisbury on the Vineyard.

On the afternoon of December 19, all was shipshape

aboard the *Globe* and she sailed once again. This day Captain Worth did not even try to make the open sea, but headed directly for Holmes' Hole for another night's anchorage. In the morning, with the early light, the sails were shaken out and she began to move. At nine o'clock the pilot was waving to them from the boat that picked him up off Cuttyhunk. The *Globe*'s big canvas was set, the wind was fresh, and they turned her out to sea, headed eastward across the Atlantic bound for the Cape Verde Islands, which marked the entrance to the whaling grounds.

The crew began to settle down. The *Globe* moved nicely in the fair wind, and before noon she passed the little island of No Mans Land, which meant the end of the Americas for many a day. The lookouts watched that bit of gray and brown disappear aft as they sailed onward in the long Atlantic swell. The anchor was stowed by now, and would not be dropped for weeks. All Captain Worth needed was to work the kinks out of his crew, to toughen the soft hands of the greenhorns and teach them the way of a ship under sail. Boys had to learn to stand a watch at the wheel and move the spokes gently so they did not overreach and cause the big square sails to flap and snap as they lost their wind in the luff. There were lurches and falterings on every watch, but at the end of three days the greenhorns had their sea legs, and the calluses were forming on their palms.

On the morning of January 1 the sky dawned bright-red, and as the captain emerged from his bunk and yawned on deck during his usual stroll, he stopped short, and made sure that First Mate Beetle had seen the signs and read them as clearly as he. They were in for a blow. For two hours it was clear and bright. The ship raced along, the blunt bows creaming the sea as they split it. But there *was* a storm brewing; even the porpoises sounded to find the shelter they could seek with their age-old knowledge of the sea.

Before noon the storm struck with breath-taking fury. The wind lashed through the rigging, screaming, and puffed the sails in sudden bursts that would have split a weaker canvas. The tarred ropes whined and the wood creaked against hemp. The ship heeled sharply, and on the lee the white spumes parted to show the light green, gray green and dark green of the depths that beckoned the mariner in a storm. Early on, every man was whisked into the rigging to clew down and shorten sail. The main topsail was close-reefed and so was the foresail, and the upper canvas was tied down. The men swung dangerously at their high posts, some sixty feet in the air, the masts seeming to mark an arc as the ship turned and moved below them. But she was a sturdy vessel and rode easily in the storm; although she heeled so that the lee rail went under, she came back each time. She scudded well.

Captain Worth was not unduly worried. He had fought storms at sea a hundred times before, and there was nothing in the performance of the *Globe* that made him anxious. As day became night, Beetle cautioned the watch officers to keep their best men at the steering lest a greenhorn panic and bring them to disaster. Men emerged from the forecastle through the hatch to slip and slide on the foam-covered decks, and feel the lines and stanchions slick with rain. Wind carried the spindrift higher than their heads, and it lashed their cheeks. In the first hours there was a flurry at the slop chest as men replaced or acquired their foul-weather gear. Whenever there was need at the slop chest there was grumbling; it did not matter how low the owners had set the prices, the men always suspected the captain of feathering his own nest. In their boots and oilskins, the men swore and prayed and worked away, watching each other anxiously to be sure that their shipmates were still there, and listening for the sounds of crackling and tearing that would mean disaster.

One trouble of the storm was that just when the men needed extra nourishment, the galley fires had to be doused. John Cleveland could not stand in his little galley without support, and to cook over flame would be to risk the most severe kind of injury, even disaster to the ship. The men were given free access (as they always had) to the ship's bread barrel, and to cold salt beef, but that was all. There were no hot, warming liquids and no stews to fill their bellies. Water and dry bread for the most of it had to suffice, as they waited for the storm to blow itself out.

When it did, at the end of two days and two nights, Captain Worth found that they had made many more sea miles than they could possibly have covered in more clement weather. Those mountainous seas that piled up behind the ship and threatened to broach over the stern at every moment had pushed the vessel in the direction he wanted to go. When the sky cleared and the sun showed brightly through wisps of white cirrus cloud, the ship dried herself out, and the weather then turned as fine as it could be. It remained fine. On January 9 the *Globe* reached the Cape Verdes, off the West African coast.

The men, of course, were hoping for shore leave with that determined optimism of sailors, but they were less than a month out of port; they had not taken a barrel of oil, and it was time to get to business, not to frolic. Captain Worth gave the islands no more than a passing glance as he turned and headed south into the old whaling grounds of years past.

3

THE BOATSTEERER

EARLY IN THE *Globe*'s voyage it had become apparent to all on board that one man was going to be a cause of trouble. He was Samuel B. Comstock, the second boatsteerer. Right away he began bullying the men of his watch and quarreling with anyone who did not agree with his forceful opinions. His position as boatsteerer was such as to give him a certain authority over all the men, and it was difficult for any to stand up to him.

Most boatsteerers chose to spend their off time with the officers of the ship in the cabin, where they "gammed" over a thousand topics, and read the books in the ship's library. Not Comstock. Except for his meals he seldom visited the cabin; he showed no sign of wanting friendship with any of the mates, and his off-hours were spent in the fo'c'sle, where he ragged the youngsters unmercifully.

But the worst of it was the way Comstock treated his watchmen. He expected his orders to be obeyed immediately, and if a greenhorn was slow, he threatened the youngster with a rope's end. Strictly speaking, this kind of discipline was not within his power, but when he had been given a watch he also had been given the responsibility of the ship's safety, and that meant he could strike a man and get away with it.

To all who knew him, it seemed odd that Comstock would be a troublemaker, for he had so much to gain from the success of the voyage and so little from its failure. Yet, Beetle was soon telling Captain Worth that Comstock *was* a troublemaker and must be watched. The captain was not pleased and did not pay much attention to his first mate's warning. He liked Comstock, and he knew Comstock both as a Nantucket man and as an experienced sailor. Worth did not know that the boatsteerer was talking against him and against the ship.

It was not just a question of Comstock's grumbling. If there was ever a whaler where grumbling did not exist, then it must have been in the seas of heaven. For as any salt of Nantucket would testify, a whaling man would sooner be deprived of his grub and his tot of rum than of the right to swear and complain.

But there was really not much to grumble about on this voyage. The *Globe* had an earned reputation as a happy ship. Captain Worth was not interfering with the men or the mates in the performance of their duty; the only general complaint against him was that when he was in a hurry he sometimes did not give them enough time to finish their meal before ordering them back to duty. But the food was good and plentiful, and there was no unusual punishment.

Comstock did not complain, but somehow he made suggestions to the others that brought about complaints. The ship was too small and the hold had been made too grand at the expense of the forecastle. The bunks were two inches too low for every man, or maybe more than that. The old man "snapped them to" too fast when he wanted the sails rerigged; he came on deck too often.

The vagueness and implausibility of many of these charges did not keep Comstock from making them. He was a strange man; even his younger brother, George, did not understand him. It was all the more odd in a Nantucketer's eyes because Comstock came from good solid Nantucket stock, and before that, equally fine New England families. One namesake, a Captain Samuel Comstock, had lived in Rhode Island and been a famous sailing man, and another namesake, his grandfather, was a judge in that state. Relatives on both sides of the family had risen to positions of prominence ashore and at sea, particularly at sea. The tradition of the whalers was also strong with the Comstocks. Indeed, through his mother's family, the Emmets of Nantucket, Boatsteerer Comstock was closely related to the Christopher Mitchell family, which dominated the whaling firm that owned the *Globe*.

Comstock was not only of sound family, then, but he was a far better-educated man than most who sailed the seas in the whaling ships. His father, Nathan Comstock, had moved to Nantucket to teach the Quaker monthly Meeting school there, and had married Elizabeth Emmet after a courtship that was looked upon favorably by Nantucket's best families. Samuel Comstock was born on the island in 1802. His mother raised the boy carefully and taught him herself. But his grandfather Samuel came to visit for a time when his grandson was very small, and he confided to the family that there was something in the boy that disturbed him. He did not know what it could be—and he was half ashamed to bring it up—but he had a strong presentiment that Samuel should stay away from the sea.

As a boy Samuel liked a joke, or what he thought was a joke, but his humor took a strange, one might say perverted, tack. He went to Meeting, of course, with his mother and father. The proceedings bored him as much as they did any young boy, and one day he laughed out loud in Meeting. All around the family, black glances fell, and women rustled their dresses in indignation.

When they reached home, Nathan Comstock chided his son for disturbing the public worship. He could not help it, young Samuel declared. Had his father not seen the presiding elder, the fattest man in Nantucket, when he fell asleep and tumbled off his bench?

No, Nathan had not seen it, and it was a marvel to him that he had not, since he was sitting within five feet of his son.

Well, that was the way it was, Samuel said: "Very strange that thee did not perceive it, for when his hat fell off it made such a clatter among the benches that several of the people stood up to see what was the matter."

Old Nathan's self-confidence was so shaken that he delayed punishment and announced that he must talk to a friend who had been sitting next to the man in question. The following day Nathan again called Samuel into the study and reported that the other man swore there had been no such occurrence.

"No wonder," Samuel said smugly, "for he was asleep, too."

So Samuel Comstock went unpunished and his father gave up the discussion altogether, for Nathan admired a boy of spirit and inventiveness, and no one could say Samuel lacked either quality. He was, in fact, precocious. One day when he was ten he stood in a store and picked up a piece of colored paper that had fallen on the floor. He turned it in his hand as the fourteen-year-old daughter of the storekeeper watched. She said he might have it if he wanted it, since it was soiled. Samuel answered that he would like it, but that it would be best if little girls did not give away things that belonged to their elders. Then he gravely put it down on the counter and walked away.

He was also stoic. Once when he and his brother William were quarreling over possession of a hammer and Samuel ended up with a split lip that had to be sewn up, he bore the pain without a cry as the doctor stitched away. It was all very odd for a child.

As a young boy Samuel was sent to a boarding school at Nine Partners in Dutchess County, New York, quite frankly because his family found him unmanageable. But he behaved badly at the boarding school, too, and after a year he was sent home. By this time Samuel refused to obey even his mother. The family moved to New York, where Samuel attended the Quaker School kept by Skipweth Cole. Cole found him impossible. Once Samuel was confined to his room as punishment. He escaped, though it cost him a sprained ankle to jump from a second-story window.

He soon joined the gang called the Downtowners, who spent their free time making mischief and quarreling with rival gangs, particularly the gang called the Corlears Hookers. A boarding school at Cedar Swamp on Long Island did no better by him; he was finally locked in the smokehouse for his misdemeanors. Even this stronghold was not proof against his ingenuity: he escaped again. Then he was sent home to New York.

He was a bright boy and good in his studies at all these schools, but he simply could not keep out of trouble; a deep hatred of any infringements on his independence was his overriding characteristic. Still, he was such a good student that his father persisted in educating him in spite of his offenses, in the hope that a college education would enable him to make a way of life for himself that he could endure.

But Samuel would have none of it. Returning for a visit to his birthplace in Nantucket, he decided that he wanted a sailor's life. Thus, when he was thirteen years old he ran away from home in New York City and went to Philadelphia, where he intended to ship out. This mischief persuaded Nathan that his son must have his own way; he granted the boy the wish to go to sea, and found him a berth on the Liverpool trader *Edward,* commanded by Captain Josiah Macy. Samuel did not return for nearly two years, during which time his mother died. He was again sent to school in New York City, this time under Goold Brown, a famous Quaker educator of the day. But he spent more time in the brothels of Lombardy Street than in class, and his friends were now the gang of boys of Corlears Hook.

A year of this, and his father tired of the boy's outright dissipations. He urged Samuel to go to sea again, but this time on a whaler. The reason was simple: whaling ships did not call at port more than necessary, and Nathan hoped that by keeping his son out of the drinking parlors, bawdy houses, and gambling dens, he might save him from the perdition to which he had apparently consigned himself. Samuel insisted that he would ship out again on a merchantman; Nathan said that unless the boy wanted to break outright with the family, his next ship would be a whaler.

So Samuel Comstock found a berth with Captain Shubael Chase, who was taking the whaler *Foster* on its maiden voyage to the Pacific. He sailed as a greenhorn before the mast, and this was the beginning of his real destiny. He took an active dislike to the mate, and a liking to two other greenhorns, John Lincoln and John Cotton. He tried to promote a cabal which involved seizing the mate and giving him a good flogging, but the others were wiser than Comstock and talked him out of it. Nonetheless, Comstock's hatred of discipline showed itself again. He was frequently heard by his friends making the most outrageous threats against the life and limb of the detested mate.

The *Foster* called at Polynesian islands, and for a few days Samuel Comstock enjoyed that heaven of sailing men around the world, fawned over by attractive *wahines,* fed new and succulent dishes, welcomed with smiles by the natives and by the swaying palm trees and the scented tropical nights. He began to think about coming back and spending his life in these islands. He would be a prince among men, he told himself. Life would be as it should be, free and open, and no need for labor to earn a few dollars and happiness. Here was wine and here were girls for the asking, all the food a man could want, and all the leisure and independence.

The idyll ended, but Samuel Comstock began to embellish his dreams as the whaler sailed south in search for its prey. He would find an island where he would be the only white. With his superior knowledge and perhaps a gun and cutlass he would be king of the island, and all who lived there would do his bidding. He would conquer other nearby islands and found an empire, and he would capture whalers like Captain Shubael Chase and set the good men free. At first John Lincoln and John Cotton listened to these tales with amusement and then with horror, which prompted them to speak to the officers about what Samuel Comstock had on his mind.

In the course of the voyage the *Foster* touched at Easter Island, and some men were allowed to go ashore. Comstock planned to desert and begin his idyll there and then. But Captain Chase refused his request to go ashore—the stories had reached him, and he firmly confined Samuel Comstock to the ship all the time they were at Easter. Comstock cursed the fate that kept him chained to the stinking, grimy sailing ship when his soul cried out for the South Seas and the fulfillment of his dreams. It was the mate's doing; somehow he knew it. Yet as the days passed, he fell into an almost somnolent mood and spoke but little to his erstwhile friends. He did his duty without complaint, but without enthusiasm or any sign that he did more than hear. When they visited Valparaiso he was allowed to go ashore, but he was not interested in the people. This was not his dream, or any part of it.

In spite of his unstable temper and constant dreaming, Samuel Comstock learned a good deal on the voyage of the *Foster*. By the time the ship was heading home, he had qualified as a boatsteerer. It took a strong brave man to wield a harpoon in an open boat; Comstock was as strong as a young bull, and his bravery was never in question.

In New York, Nathan Comstock had forsaken teaching for the more remunerative life of a merchant. Samuel came into town and to the family house with as much insouciance as if he had never left. Before the first day was over he was flirting with a young New York lady and talking wildly of marriage. His sister noticed this, and a change in her brother wrought by the voyage in the Pacific. "He has a bad look about him," she told William, who expressed an even stronger opinion that the sea had changed his brother for the worse: a strange look in Samuel's eyes bothered him. "There was a deep subtle and mysterious expression about them which I thought very repulsive," he said.

The whole family was distressed by Samuel's erratic behavior these days, and all hoped that he would somehow snap out of this state of mind, in which he did very little but chase girls and tell wild stories of the sea. His father suggested that Samuel forsake the sea altogether in view of this unhealthy effect, and Samuel agreed, or seemed to. His father then offered Samuel a position in his business. The young man was sent to supervise the movement of merchandise into a new store which the elder Comstock had bought.

When Samuel and his brother William visited the store they found the place empty except for a pretty mulatto girl who was busy whitewashing the walls. Samuel took a good look, then he called her over and ordered her to go down the cellar and fetch a pail of water.

The girl did as she was told. In a moment Samuel excused himself and opened the cellar door, stepped down and closed it firmly behind him.

William stood in the silent room, listening to the noises of the street, uncomfortable, waiting for Samuel and the girl to reappear. They were gone for what seemed an hour, and then they came up, Samuel with a thin smile on his face. The girl went back to her whitewashing without a word, but a bit later when William chanced by where she was working, she looked at him half triumphantly and laughed. "That brother of yours is a real devil," she said.

There was one girl after another. Something about the devil-may-care look on Samuel's face brought otherwise respectable young women to actions their families would hardly countenance. He took one mistress after another, and usually more than one at a time. He promised them anything; William knew that Samuel was "engaged" to at least three or four girls and that he talked confidently to each of them of their coming marriage.

Samuel's behavior continued to be inexplicable to his family. One moment he was bragging about his seduction of a shopgirl, the next he was talking of his plans to join a ship, kill the captain and capture the vessel, and sail to his South Sea island. He became more vehement about this as time passed.

He had tried one way of achieving his dream: jump ship at a tropic isle. Bt just as Captain Shubael Chase had thwarted that ambition, it was likely that any captain would try to cross him again. So his plans were changed; it was no longer enough to sail to the South Seas and leave the ship. He would have to stage a mutiny in order to be able to do as he was bound to do.

Brother William did not believe that these ideas were any more than delusions of grandeur. They were of a piece with the tales Samuel told about his adventures and the yarns he spun to intrigue the girls. They were not always the same tales, and the strange notion of becoming king of a tropical isle was only one of them. In a few brief months Samuel made a dozen statements about his plans for the future. There was nothing the family could do but wait and see.

William went off to Nantucket to continue the old family tradition of whaling, but Samuel repeated his promise that he would never again serve aboard a ship. His father was pleased and hoped that the young man would settle down in the mercantile business in New York and succeed him.

For several months Samuel appeared happy enough with the merchant's life. His father was talking about buying ships and setting up in the Atlantic trade, and Samuel began to think of himself as a shipping owner. That reasoning needed only a small step to lead to the notion that he might take a ship out himself—not a whaler, of course, but a regular merchantman. But he must learn a good deal more than he knew about the art of seamanship and the science of navigation.

Samuel's path led him to the Brooklyn wharf, where the U.S. Navy frigates called for their provisioning. Soon he was admiring the bearing of the officers of the bright young American navy. He saw this as life as a gentleman at sea, defending his country's honor against Barbary pirates and any others who challenged American trade rights or insulted the nation's flag. He began studying navigation and became fairly proficient. He studied medicine and surgery and bought a surgical outfit, on the pretentious theory that his first command would be too small a vessel to boast a surgeon, and that he must therefore be able to treat his men's ailments and injuries.

His father was not pleased. To have a son join the colors was the very antithesis of the Quaker faith; in the recent revolution, Quakers of Pennsylvania had balked at paying taxes to Congress to support war; in the War of 1812 they had remained quiescent and refused to have anything to do with the struggle. Samuel's plans brought Nathan to such a pitch of emotion that he forbade him to join the service of his country.

One of the strange contradictory streaks of Samuel Comstock's nature now revealed itself again. Many a young man deciding on a career would tell the family to mind their own business and go hang if they did not like the decision. But Samuel bowed meekly to his father's will and gave up the place made for him aboard the frigate. He came back to the store, but was so moody and negative that Nathan Comstock soon advised the young man to get away and find himself another profession. Storekeeping was obviously not for Samuel.

Samuel elected to go awhaling once again. Under the circumstances, Nathan was pleased and hoped his wayward son had finally found himself. If Samuel would go awhaling and would comport himself as a whaling man should, Nathan promised that then, when he came home from his next voyage, Nathan would, after making sure that he had an adequate knowledge of navigation, buy a whaling vessel and set Samuel up in business for himself.

The offer should have seemed overwhelmingly inviting to any young man of Samuel's spirit, and it appeared to attract the young sailor completely. He took himself to Nantucket and found a berth as boatsteerer with Captain Gardner on the *Globe*. If he had to go "blubber hunting" again, he could not have chosen a luckier ship. More, with his father's promise behind him, he seemed to want to do just what he was doing.

After a few days in Nantucket, Samuel returned to New York to pick up his possessions. His younger brother, George, begged to go along on the voyage. Nathan, who now had high hopes that Samuel was on the right track, saw nothing amiss in George's request. If Nathan was to go into the whaling trade, then it was the natural thing for George to learn it too. So Nathan gave his consent, and the two Comstock brothers made ready to head for Nantucket and their ship, Samuel assuring his father and brother that there would be no trouble in getting George signed on.

George was a bit surprised at what Samuel decided to take with them. Samuel bought a lot more clothes than George had ever thought were necessary, particularly cotton clothing. He also bought a new set of surgical instruments, a complete medicine chest and seeds. When George asked why his brother wanted such a curious lot of equipment, he got no answer.

When the Comstock brothers reached Nantucket, Samuel first went to see First Mate Worth, whom he had met earlier, when he signed on. Those two had hit it off marvelously from the beginning, and that explains Samuel's airy assurances to his father and brother that George would have no trouble getting a berth on the *Globe*.

There was no trouble. Young George was signed on as an apprentice seaman without ado. He went to the ship and began learning all the secrets of a strange new world while brother Samuel and Mate Worth made the rounds of the taverns together, courting young women of easy disposition, and got along famously.

When Worth was suddenly appointed captain of the vessel, Samuel Comstock was surprised and shocked. He had never thought of First Mate Worth as becoming Captain Worth. He was uneasy, yet in those pleasant days in Nantucket none of this uneasiness was allowed to show.

Even when the ship moved down to Martha's Vineyard for refitting and provisioning, Mate Worth and Boatsteerer Comstock had been much in one another's company. Since Worth was a Vineyard man, he knew everyone on the island that counted in the whaling trade, so Comstock gained entrée to those circles. When Worth married in the early autumn, Comstock became a favorite of the first mate's bride and she was as quick as anyone to smile at his repartee.

Early in the voyage of the *Globe,* Captain Worth's favoritism for Comstock was so noticeable that the officers and Boatsteerer Smith commented on it. They admired Worth and his accomplishments, and they did not understand his attachment to a man they found so formidable. One thing was certain, Comstock had the same way of managing men that Worth had shown as a mate; he was tough as nails. Perhaps that was their bond, the officers decided. But as captain, Worth was unexceptionable. He did not interfere with Beetle's daily management of the ship any more than he would have wanted Captain Gardner to interfere with his. Nothing was unusual except for his strange attachment to the boatsteerer. The two were often seen yarning together on the after deck in the softening light of the first dogwatch. The officers did not like it, and they let Comstock know in a dozen different little ways. So Comstock took to spending even more of his time in the forecastle. If he was not totally popular there, it did not seem to disturb him. He did his duty, and he gammed with the men.

4

"THAR SHE BLOWS!"

THE VOYAGE was uneventful for weeks, although the ship was in whaling water and might expect to encounter a spout at any time. They were sailing through the old whaling grounds south of the equator. It was not surprising that they did not see any whales, for in recent years the luck had not been nearly so good here as in the past. Still, there was always a chance, and for a month Captain Worth sailed a crooked course in the hope of finding spouts. Nothing.

Then one day the lookout in the foretop sang out: "Sail ho."

It was not the call for whale but something almost as exciting, another ship. The *Globe* was a scarce two months at sea, but that made no difference. A ship in these grounds called for a gam. There was the pleasure of meeting another captain and crew, of course, and among whalers from North America this often meant relatives or friends. There was also the very real exchange of information that might bring Captain Worth the luck he sought.

Mate Beetle, who was on deck when the sail was sighted, ran below to rouse the captain. The watch sent a man forward to tell the men in the forecastle. The word seeped into the steerage, and in five minutes all the ship's complement was on deck, peering over the bulwarks, men moving into the futtocks to see better.

As they spotted the other vessel, so her crew saw them, and soon the ships were traveling on converging courses. The other might be an Englishman or a Dutchman, even a Spaniard; but in these latitudes, far off the shipping lanes, she was most likely to be a whaler, and a whaler from home.

In two hours the ships were almost bow to stern. The captain of the other ship was quick to move. He got his boat in the water and headed toward the *Globe.* Thus he won the right to come visiting, to get his feet off his own deck and shuck the eternal responsibility for a few hours while he and Captain Worth talked about the affairs of shore and sea. It was as good as a vacation.

And so it was, too, for the men. For in two months all the newness had worn off the old stories, even for the greenhorns. The sounds of the fiddle were so familiar in the fo'c'sle that anything new would be welcome, and another ship would bring a different pattern of talk and music, even grumbling. The crews eagerly changed over, about half the men of the *Enterprise* —for that was their visitor's name—coming to the *Globe,* while half the latter ship's crew made the reverse voyage. The officers changed over, too.

First Mate Beetle and Second Mate Lumbert went over to the *Enterprise.* The captain, Third Mate Fisher and the two boatsteerers did the honors for the *Globe* on her decks. The rum was broken out for a little tot, and the cook did himself proud with a special duff. So it was a day of festivity as the ships rolled gently in the pleasant tropical sea, only a few cable lengths from each other. In the excitement of it, someone proposed that they have wrestling matches aboard the *Globe.*

Usually such contests were ship against ship. But today—perhaps it was the rum, which seemed to make Samuel Comstock choleric, as it always did, or perhaps it was some fancied slight of the past, or it might have been the sea air in these climes or simply the deviltry of it—whatever the cause, Comstock went quite against tradition and challenged his own third mate to a contest of skill and strength.

A cry went up on deck. Fisher weighed a good forty pounds more than the middle-sized boatsteerer and was half a head taller. He shook his head and told Samuel Comstock to forget it. But Comstock's stubborn streak was aroused. He said he wanted to wrestle Fisher, and, by God, unless Fisher was a coward, they would wrestle. He began to strip off his shirt.

That was the kind of challenge no man dared resist. Fisher looked about the deck, helplessly. The others were silent, warned by the insistence of Comstock's demand. So Fisher shrugged as if to shake off all his officer's responsibility and removed his shirt also.

Samuel Comstock came upon him, neck sunk deep down in the collarbones of his wide frame, arms out at the elbows, hands ready to grasp. He was, for his moderate size, a well-developed man, strong and balanced, with knotted triceps and biceps which showed the use of the harpoon and the flensing spade.

Fisher stood up straight and let him come. Samuel grabbed, reaching for Fisher's head, but the big mate thrust his arms around the smaller man and embraced him in a bear hug. He pulled once and then let Comstock fall.

The sound of laughter echoed across the water. Fisher was relaxed. He looked over at Comstock as if to say, "There, you've had your fun. Now let's get down to gamming."

But Samuel Comstock's fury was fully aroused. He came charging up off the deck at the third mate. Fisher picked up Comstock by crotch and collarbone and bounced him on the oak deck. Almost immediately the big man regretted it and stood aside as if to end the affair. He did not look happy.

Comstock was black with fury now, but he had the good sense to stay down. Even so, Fisher and some of the other men of the *Globe* heard him threaten bloody vengeance on the man who had bested him.

After this disagreeable event, Captain Worth and Mate Fisher moved aft with the captain of the *Enterprise* and his officers while Comstock got hold of his temper. But those who stayed behind to watch him saw that he had not put the matter aside ten minutes later—as Fisher had obviously done. And any who were watching Samuel Comstock as closely as his brother George were puzzled. Something desperate was overtaking the man.

In spite of the unpleasantness with Samuel Comstock, the gam between the ships was a success, and soon the two crews sailed away with renewed vigor to pursue their long, separate, lonely journeys into better hunting territory.

A few days later Captain Worth's decisions to follow the routine path was rewarded, for from aloft, just before noon, came the long-awaited cry: "Thar she blows!"

Captain Worth rushed from his stateroom through the cabin and out onto deck, not quite dressed but ready to give the order that would send the boats into motion. He looked aloft and asked the lookout for all the details he could get about the spouting—size, number, frequency—and the flukes that could be seen, if any.

It was only one whale, but on a day like this, so far out and so long at sea without a single barrel of oil in the hold, Captain Worth was not going to turn down anything.

This was the moment the boat crews had been waiting for. During the previous weeks they had trained hard in good weather, chasing a spar the captain towed well behind the stern, and the greenhorns had learned what it meant to spring into action. Soon the boats went down with a splash, for even with main yard hauled back, the ship was making a good four knots and the apparently sensitive little whaleboats bounced in the froth-capped water next to the ship.

Samuel Comstock was as excited as the next man. There was a fervor to this moment that could not be denied—the excitement of the chase, when each crew of oarsmen would chal-

lenge the other two crews. Second Mate Lumbert was the officer
in command of Comstock's waist boat. Mate Beetle and Boatsteerer Smith took the larboard boat. The starboard boat got
away first, which brought a wide grin to Captain Worth's face—
the "old man" was still good for a kick or two. But Comstock
shouted and cursed and doubled up his fist, so that his men
flinched as they moved, but they quickly overhauled the captain, who had the disadvantage of coming around to larboard
as the whales—now more were in sight—moved away from the
ship. The man in the crosstrees sang out.

Lumbert sculled the steering oar to help them speed toward
the whales. It was a rough day on the sea, with the wind
blowing so hard that John Cleveland had called it half a gale—
but then, Cookie was always prone to exaggerate. Still, the spew
of the waves was in their faces, and the oarsmen must watch carefully not to catch a crab as the boat surged up and down through
the water. Looking sharply, Comstock saw several whales and
moved in the boat to catch Lumbert's attention. They were going
for Beetle.

The three cockleshells raced across the water, propelled by
willing, burning hands, until the men standing in bow and
stern could see clearly the spouts of condensed moisture that
emerged from the blowholes of the great whales. Then the
beasts stopped blowing and coasted, moving along just below
the surface, steadily, apparently without noticing the tiny shells
that chased them.

The chase continued for half an hour. Every ten minutes or so
the whales came up to blow, then disappeared. It was on such a
blow that the men had to act quickly, or lose the prize. Still they
were too far away.

After another steady half-hour of rowing, the panting men
stopped for a while. They half lay, chests heaving, over their
oars. Then they dashed on and seemed to gain, but the whales
"turned flukes," almost in unison, and went down, down,
down before the boats could reach them. The men stopped;

disgust crossed one face and then another, and they rested, once more, panting on the oars.

They waited.

When spouts showed again, the spumes were far of; the whales had milled—changed course—while under water and had outrun them. There was precious little chance that they could catch even one whale this day.

The glory of chase died, flat. When Lumbert looked up at the sky for the first time, he whistled. A black cloud was moving in low on them, and that meant squall, which could be vicious in a cockleshell of a whaleboat in the Atlantic, winter or summer. The fact that they were below the equator and that summer was just drifting into fall did not mean a thing. As the men of Comstock's boat were waiting there for a moment, and those of the other two boats did the same, the cloud moved in on them and the wind freshened. So they all headed home to their ship, listless, spirits dashed by the loss of the whales that had seemed so attainable, for just that moment.

Then came a shout: "Thar she blooooooows!"

Sure enough, off to the starboard of the little fleet a single spout showed—one lone straggler, left behind by the school when something—some sonar emanation, some sound—had frightened the others and sent them milling off.

The boats sped forward. In the bow of each a boatsteerer poised his harpoon. The crew of Comstock's boat gave the final backbending surge that sent one whaleboat ahead of the other, and with a great thrust Comstock sent his shaft into the side of the whale before the next boat could. The whale grunted audibly, a bursting gout of blood welling from the harpoon hole. Then it was flukes up, and the monster slid beneath the water.

The Nantucket sleigh ride began, albeit this was a short one. The whale soon surfaced, spouting blood through his blow holes. In fifteen minutes the beast turned on his side and lay panting. He was still for a minute or two, and then he died, mouth gaping open to show the great double row of teeth in the lower jaw that marked him unmistakably as a sperm.

The two other boat crews turned to help. Soon three harpoons were in the dead whale, attached to three lines, and the boats towed the carcass back to the ship.

The squall that had endangered the whaleboats had passed by the ship, without causing any trouble. Even though it was nearly dark, the men boarded the ship, grabbed a quick bite and then set about the clearing of the blubber and the trying out of the oil that was the purpose of the voyage.

Now the reason why the men lived below the main deck of a whaler became obvious. Except for the two hatches that led below and the helmsman's cockpit, the whole main deck was given to whale butchering and boiling of blubber into oil, for the barrels that would be stored below. With a whale alongside, the work ahead was prodigious.

5

TRYING OUT

IF THE *Globe* had been unlucky in missing the rest of the school of whales, thus dashing Captain Worth's hopes of finding five or six hundred barrels of oil in one day's work, still, the weather stayed good as the great blubbery carcass rode along, the eye amidships, on the starboard side of the ship. The big flukes dragged past the after section, for the whale was nearly as long as the *Globe*.

Because the weather was so fine, the sense of urgency died down that night, and the flensing and boiling were put aside until the next morning. At dawn all hands were piped to the quarter deck and the captain gave a speech about the need for absolute cooperation and obedience in the factory end of whaling. Then came the preparations of "cutting in."

Mate Beetle supervised the attaching of a fluke rope. A snake line was thrown over the whale, attached to a lead so that the line would sink, and to a block of wood. The lineman threw the line at an angle, so the lead went to the bottom between the whale and the ship, the wood bobbed up, was retrieved, and the men of the *Globe* had a fluke line around the whale. Soon this line was replaced by an eight-inch howser attached to block and tackle, and these to a ship's boom on the foremast, for the whale was turned around so that the flukes were forward and the head aft, on the weather side of the ship. This was to prevent the whale from striking the ship, falling off and striking again, which might break up the ship's timbers.

The *Globe* had lain tight-reefed during the night, but this morning Captain Worth ordered the reefs shaken out so that she would sail slow and easy—the ship's progress keeping the head of the animal from drifting out at right angles to the side. That big body had to be up against the ship so the work could be done.

The duty of Third Mate Fisher and the two boatsteerers was to cut away the flesh of the whale—the blubber that was wanted —and get it ready for the try-pots. They alternated, depending on whose whale it was, in the duty of fastening the blubber hook. This meant that the man who had the task went over the side onto the whale's back; above him stood the two others, each holding a flensing spade on a sixteen-foot pole, each standing on a narrow stage slung over the side of the ship and secured by lines.

Dressed in a woolen suit and long woolen stockings to give him some traction on the slippery animal, the man on the whale then slid down, often falling into the water and being hauled back up onto the beast's back, as another cut a round piece out of the "white horse" around the eye and then made a semicircular cut above, to create a flap four feet wide. This was the beginning of the peeling of the whale, a process very much like the peeling of an orange, with the men with the spades cutting loose the strip of blubber on two sides, and the block and tackle pulling the blubber off against the weight of the carcass in the water.

There was no getting away from this work. For captain and owners and for the rest it was the payoff, and no man dared shirk his part in it. Once the hook was in place, and the blubber was peeling away, only half the battle was won. There remained the cutting up of the blubber into pieces small enough for the iron try-pots, and the continual flensing away of the fat from the body.

As the blubber moved ever upward, eventually it reached

the block and tackle on the mast, and the mate then announced "To blocks"—which meant the blubber was up to the blocks, as high as it could go, and the windlass must be stopped until the boatsteerers took up boarding knives and cut off the piece of blubber and started again below, with a new eye and a new roll.

These boarding knives were wicked, dangerous instruments. They were sharp as razors for their task, double-edged and pointed, with four-foot blades and three-foot handles. Only with such an implement could even a strong man cut through the eight-inch-thick layer of blubber before him.

At the order "To blocks" the boatsteerer cut out an oval plug from the middle of the blubber sheet, and the hook of the second block and tackle was thrust through. The cutter then slashed away at the blubber above the new eye, and the piece was cut off. That was Comstock's work—the most gory and blubbery of all.

While the blubber was being stripped, Captain Worth stood aft on another stage, undertaking the operation of cutting off the head of the beast. He cut through three feet of dark coarse-fibered muscle—through tendons as large as cables, and blood vessels so big a dog could be pushed through them. Finally Worth's long spade reached the place where the head joined the vertebrae and he cut through. He saw the whale secured to chains, and then went to the try-pots amidships to be sure they were lit and getting ready for the stinking task of boiling. The corpse was sent floating on its lumbering way, trailing blood and fluids, while sharks and gulls and the albatrosses swarmed about, snatching morsels from the dead creature.

Then the mates and men turned their attention to the head. It was a sperm whale, so the spermaceti, that finest of oils, was to be found in the head cavities, and, in all, the men of the *Globe* managed to dip out nearly twenty barrels from this whale. This was a pleasant, unguent oil, nothing like the blubbery substance bubbling in the try-pots, and the men reveled in the soft feel of it on their blistered and work-worn hands. All but Samuel Comstock. He detested the butchery and he was in a fury during it. His brother heard him say that he'd be damned if he was going to be a cursed blubber hunter all his life.

After the incident of the whale, Comstock became more irritable. He said the whale oil had a bad effect, and that it was "filling him with biles and inflaming the flesh." Perhaps. It certainly made a tiger of him. Speaking to George and writing home, he lamented that he had been persuaded not to take that berth in the frigate. His father's false promises had ruined his whole life, he said.

He was so upset that he could not sleep, so he turned even more to his books, working twenty hours out of the twenty-four for ship and self. He became an insufferable watchkeeper; if he found one of his watchmen asleep on duty, he would pour seawater over him. The first time he did this it was considered a joke. But the waist-boat watch quickly tired of the joke, and of his unbending demand for attention and discipline.

Before February was out, the resentment in the waist-boat watch was apparent to every man aboard the ship. Comstock was a "real spitfire" said one of his men—and that was no compliment in Nantucket terms, for it meant he was one who took advantage of a bit of authority to tyrannize his companions unmercifully. Something was going to have to give soon.

6

RESTLESS DAYS

BOATSTEERER COMSTOCK was difficult for anyone aboard the *Globe* to fathom. As far as Captain Worth was concerned, it now seemed that Comstock could do no wrong; when more complaints about harsh treatment of his watch continued to reach Worth through Second Mate Lumbert, the most kindly of officers, the captain frowned and told Lumbert to mind his own stays. There was nothing wrong with a little discipline, the captain said, and he announced that he continued to be well pleased with Comstock's zeal in behalf of the ship and that some of the officers could profit by watching the boat-steerer.

Constant Lewis was in trouble with Comstock from the very first. He was slow and arrogant and refused to answer when called. He mounted the shrouds like an old lady going up the church steps, and he talked back to Comstock every time he was given a direct order.

The first time Captain Worth heard Lewis sounding off, he grabbed the seaman by the throat the way a farmer grabs a turkey, picked up the nearest lashing and quirted him with it half a dozen times, then told him to mind his sea manners. The second time Captain Worth's attention was aroused by Lewis' slackness, he ordered Mr. Beetle up and told him to

43

43

put the man in irons. So Lewis was manacled by hand and chains were put on his ankles, and he was thrust into the chain locker forward to meditate on his sins.

As far as the captain was concerned, this discipline was not considered anything out of the norm. A captain had to maintain order. The men before the mast sympathized with Lewis, but they knew he was a shirker. So it was with Cook Cleveland. He was a good enough fellow, but when the captain gave him a flogging for being drunk, the men understood it. No, as far as the ship was concerned, the *Globe* was a happy ship, except for Comstock's watch, which now became known openly as "the spitfire watch."

George Comstock escaped the brunt because he was related to the tyrant; Comstock was not trying to drive him either to action or to desertion, which he was obviously trying to do with the other men of the watch. But while it was hard on Seamen Ingham, Cook and Lewis, it was even harder on young Prass because he was a foreigner and a Roman Catholic. These men began to spend most of their off-duty hours among themselves, as if they were licking wounds, speaking quietly in whispers and exchanging knowing looks.

Within three months of the beginning of the voyage, Comstock had also made an enemy of John Cleveland. Cleveland sympathized with the men on Comstock's watch and was not above speaking his mind. Comstock told him to go to his grandmother or the devil, he did not care which. A dangerous light dawned in Cook Cleveland's eye.

Their mutual dislike grew, and on one occasion Captain Worth stepped in to stop an argument between them. Worth promised the cook another taste of the rope's end if he did not leave the boatsteerer alone. Again Worth was interceding for Samuel Comstock—which did not go unnoticed in the fo'c'sle.

And yet Comstock was not really unpopular; he was held in respect for his ability to manipulate the captain. The others did not know that Comstock and Captain Worth had spent many hours before Worth's appointment by the Mitchells, talking over how Worth would outdo his predecessor if he had the job. Comstock was not only Worth's friend, but therefore he also knew more about the course of the voyage they were taking than any other man on board. When Worth spent but little time in the old northern whaling grounds and then headed south, Comstock knew why. And as Captain Worth made but a short run through southern grounds, Comstock also knew why.

Worth intended to continue the experiment that Captain Gardner had carried out so successfully on the last voyage of the *Globe*. Gardner had taken the ship to the mysterious Japanese islands and there had found whaling so good that he had vowed to return there on the next voyage. Worth was doing no more than carrying out that promise. So now, as Comstock knew he would, Worth headed straight for Hawaii (called Sandwich Islands then), for that was the shortest route to the Orient. He would stop there—Comstock knew that, too— in order to obtain the latest information about the whaling prospects.

Early in March, the *Globe* approached Cape Horn, and the preparations for rounding it began. All the spars above the topmast were ordered down. Captain Worth was taking no chances at all with these waters, for he knew them well and he was perfectly aware of the dangers these currents and winds posed for sailing ships. Once First Mate Beetle had supervised the unshipping of the upper spars, Mate Lumbert was put to work below stowing the bow anchors so they would be neither lost in a blow nor pushed so as to smash the ship and become dangerous to life. The anchor stocks were removed and the big iron hooks were lashed securely to the ring bolts in the deck forward. The boats were all taken off their davits, and secured on deck over the spars and yards and topmast spares. Everything above deck that could possibly slide or smash was double-lashed. The try-pots and the blubber-cutting tables were strengthened with spars and lashings.

At the end of the day Captain Worth inspected what had

been done. With a cool, cautious eye he looked around to see if there were any loose ends that might be sent flapping in the gales or even hurricane winds he could expect at any time on this perilous passage.

The winds were growing colder and more erratic; the whole crew noticed it. A few days before, they had been dressed in cottons, and now they were wearing heavy woolen sweaters and sou'westers. This was iceberg country, and the watch was warned, although there did not seem to be any icebergs around in this season. But Staten Island and the smaller rocks in the Strait of Le Maire made navigation hazardous. At some points the breakers seemed to lie half a mile offshore, a sure sign of hidden reefs. The very real fear was that current and wind, combined with the blindness of a heavy squall, might cause the ship to founder or run up on a rocky, deserted coast.

That was the way they moved down upon "Cape Stiff," as the sailors called the Horn. But Captain Worth was as lucky as he had ever been. The whaler slipped almost effortlessly around Cape Horn on March 5, without even a blow that could be called a gale, and headed north into a tranquil Pacific Ocean.

March sped by. No whales. Captain Worth had not really expected to encounter any schools on the course he took, but the men, who were not consulted on route or plans, could not understand why their captain had deserted the old grounds. Worth, as the men now remembered audibly, was an untried factor. It was one thing to be mate of a successful whaling vessel under a captain who knew precisely what he was doing. It was quite another matter for that same mate to be shoved into command early, without being dry behind the ears.

Any who questioned Worth's judgment, and there were some in the fo'c'sle who now did, had no way of reckoning with the captain's full plans. For the Japanese islands were dangerous territory. For centuries the emperors and shoguns of Japan had forbidden their people to have contact with foreigners. A handful of Dutch and Portuguese had landed in Japan, but many of them had been killed, some had been sent home and some had been held prisoner. Worth knew that he could not land in Japan, or in the surrounding territory. It was doubly dangerous then: not only did he face all the hazards of the sea but in those waters he was surrounded by human enemies.

Samuel Comstock was excited by the direction in which Captain Worth was traveling. He continued his hard, driving work and his relentless study of scientific subjects, and no one, even his brother, dared ask him why he did these things. For when others asked what he was reading he was evasive, and when George caught sight of a text on astronomy and asked straight out what good it was, Samuel simply smiled and said he'd find out.

The closer they came to Hawaii, the more jovial Comstock became; in fact, the seamen began to find him almost likeable. But he continued to be as harsh as ever with his own watchmen. He ignored Boatsteerer Smith and the officers, but he had no quarrels among the other men. He achieved a certain begrudging acclaim with everyone aboard for his superior medical knowledge. When one of the men suffered from kidney stones, Samuel brought forth his black medical chest and found a vial with a powder in it that made the stone pass. The sufferer swore it did, anyhow, and that he had no further pain.

While on watch one day Comstock hurt his foot on a boarding knife that had been left carelessly on the deck. The gash on the instep became infected and he found it hard to stand watch. The foot swelled and reddened. Another might have gone to the captain, who was always the surgeon general of a sailing ship, but Comstock chose to treat himself. In his sea chest he found the surgical set he had purchased in New York. He commanded young Prass to stand by with a fish hook attached to a string to hold the wound open, and while the fascinated youth watched, Comstock took up a lancet and split the flesh of his foot laterally along the instep from ankle to big toe, down to the bone. Blood spurted forth on the deck and Prass flinched.

"What's wrong, boy, are you a coward?" the boatsteerer asked as he picked up a scraper and tore the flesh and infection to the bone, until satisfied that he had reached the seat of the trouble. Then, calmly, as Prass nearly fainted from the sight of exposed tendons, veins and bleeding flesh, Comstock sewed up his own foot with the precision of a sailmaker and put a rough woolen sock on it. He hobbled about for a few days, the swelling healed and he was as good as new. Again, this performance brought a grudging respect from the men of the ship.

April came and still no whales, and the crew grew more restive than ever. One day in the last week of the month, when the afternoon sun hung low on the horizon, young Seaman William Lay, who was in the crosstrees, suddenly sang out: "Thar she blows—blooooooows!"

And once again all the activity of the first sighting was repeated. Captain Worth was on deck in a moment, shouting, searching and running into the rigging. This time the whales were a good ten miles away, and had their spouts not been reflected in the dying rays of the long-reaching sun, Lay might not have seen them at all. The wind was against the ship, the time of day was against them and Captain Worth had to make his decision. The wind was carrying them swiftly toward the Sandwiches, where he wanted to go. Should they turn and give chase, moving far off their course? If they chased, there was little they could do that night. The moon was new and the sea would be dark; their chances of making a night catch were almost infinitesimal. By next morning the whales could have milled a half-dozen times beneath the surface and be completely out of touch with the ship. And they would have lost precious days to no avail.

No. Captain Worth was not risking time now for a bare chance at more barrels of blubber. He wanted to be on the Japan station and he wanted to get there quickly. He looked up into the shrouds and ordered young Lay to stop calling out.

The men on deck looked at one another, puzzled. They did not understand their captain at all these days.

That was at the end of April. The morning of May 1 dawned bright and sunny, and before nine o'clock the lookout shouted: "Land ho!"

Again every man rushed to the deck and the captain was at the foot of the foremast. He had expected to make the landfall of the Hawaiian Islands early that day—and he had.

All day the land stayed alongside as they tacked to reach Oahu. Late in the afternoon young seaman Lay in the crosstrees again sang out: "Thar she blows!"

Now, that *was* a puzzler. The captain was amazed. Whales here so close to land? It could be, of course—anything could happen at sea. But the captain wanted more information before he became excited. "What whale and where?" he demanded.

It was a school, said young Lay; he could see them coming toward the ship.

Captain Worth leaped into the shrouds and hauled himself up a good ten feet. He balanced and steadied his glass with one hand. He looked, focused and looked again. Then he snapped the glass close and jumped down. It was all right, he said kindly to the apprentice seaman. Something was there, but it was canoes, not whales.

Captain Worth then called First Mate Beetle to give him instructions about contact with the natives. There could be trade, and all the natives would be allowed aboard. He knew from the past the habits of the islanders: they came to a ship and swarmed over it like bees, touching, smelling, enjoying the strangeness of the sailing craft. But no women would be allowed below deck, and no women would be allowed to stay aboard overnight. That was a firm order.

The men were so pleased at the prospect of trade and leave ashore that they did not complain. Soon the brown-skinned Kanakas from the canoes were swarming about the deck of the

whaler, laughing and holding up their treasures. There were potatoes, yams, fish, coconuts and a squealing young pig to be
bought. The captain looked and ordered half a dozen pigs—big
ones—for the ship's mess. The cook began trading for fresh fruit
and vegetables. The men began bartering on their own.

Cooper Coffin and Assistant Cooper Cyrus Hussey had a
busy day. Mate Beetle ordered them to build a pigpen forward of the foremast, and before nightfall they had finished it
so the natives could deliver half a dozen squealing hogs of
various sizes. They settled in and began rooting among the
palm leaves the natives had brought for bedding.

From below, the crew brought up rum, even though they
knew Captain Worth would frown on it. Soon the fiddle was
playing and the native drums were pounding on deck, and the
ship rang with the sounds of happy laughter. Halfway through
the evening Beetle shooed the natives overboard, and reluctantly
they went, men and bare-breasted girls in tapa skirts leaping over
the side and swimming like porpoises to their canoes. Half an
hour later the ship had settled down for the night.

In the morning Beetle came on deck to inspect the watch and
to make sure that all the debris of the previous evening was
over the side. Then he saw a bronzed back of an obviously female figure parading on the main deck between the try-pots and
the mainmast. She was wearing precious little but a tiny neth-
er garment and a Scotch bonnet on her head. She giggled and
pulled at a pair of rose blankets, the other end of them held
by a grinning, teasing Comstock.

Beetle was furious. He stared and he shouted at Comstock
and they quarreled over the boatsteerer's violation of the captain's specific order. Then Comstock turned his back on the
mate, who went off to inform the captain that the boatsteerer
had a woman aboard.

The captain did not take the breach of discipline at all the
way Beetle thought he should. In fact, he was on deck and had
seen the confrontation, and by the time Beetle reached him he

obviously made up his mind not to be aroused. He nodded and quietly told Beetle to break out a boat and take the young woman ashore. But he offered no solution to the disciplinary problem posed by Comstock, except to tell Beetle that he would take care of it himself.

So another puzzle was added to the picture. The incident raised Comstock's standing with the crew considerably, and it did not seem to hurt his position on the ship. What strange hold did he have on the captain that he could defy the orders of the night and yet emerge unscathed next day?

7

JUMPING SHIP

THAT DAY the trading continued. The natives came out again
with canoes laden with more potatoes, sugar canes, bananas,
and fish that the coopers flung into barrels while Cook
Cleveland supervised the salting down, rubbing his hands betweentimes on the tattered gray garment that he still called an
apron. The women had all disappeared and did not show
up again, warned off by Mate Beetle as he brought Samuel
Comstock's lady of the night back to Hawaii's shore.

Late in the day the ship was fully provisioned with fresh
goods from the island of Hawaii, and the pigs were grunting
lustily as they devoured their meal of yams. Grinning and waving, the natives took back with them pieces of iron hoop, nails,
hammers and cheap trade goods. The hoops they regarded most
highly of all, for they would make knives and swords and jewelry.

The *Globe* sailed then for Oahu's Diamond Head, where the
great natural harbor lay. Inside Pearl Harbor the ship pulled up
between the *Palladium,* a whaler out of Boston, and the *Poca-
hontas,* another out of Falmouth. The chains rattled as the
anchor went overboard into the deep water of the bay.

Much as the men hoped for shore leave, Captain Worth did
not grant it. First he called on his fellow masters of the two whalers and agreed with them that they should sail out of the harbor

in convoy and head for the Japanese whaling grounds. Then he
went ashore to pay his respects to the missionaries who had established themselves in the islands about three years earlier. He
called on the Reverend Hiram Bingham, the leader of the fiery
Protestants, who with his wife kept a school in Honolulu. Captain Worth was back before midnight and gave orders that they
would sail in the morning with the other two whalers. Comstock was notably crestfallen. All his good temper of the past
weeks evaporated and he grew sullen and standoffish. Something was bothering him.

So the ships sailed, less than twenty-four hours after the
shadow of Diamond Head had fallen on the decks of the *Globe*.
For two days they sailed together. Then the *Palladium* pulled
away, to follow her captain's bent, and the next day the *Poca-
hontas* left them. Whaling was a highly competitive business,
and one best carried out alone.

For the first two weeks Cook Cleveland managed to keep the
fresh vegetables and fruits edible by dousing them in salt water.
But soon after, the crew was back on the diet of salt beef, salt
pork, dried beans and ship's bread, with an occasional coconut
as long as they lasted. The pigs were first fed on yams, and when
the yams were gone they ate ship's bread.

For some reason these pigs irritated Samuel Comstock more
than anything or anyone else aboard the *Globe*. He would walk
up on the forecastle of an evening and look at them and shake
his head in disgust, calling them "damn hogs." One night while
he was on watch and the rest of the ship was presumably asleep,
the pigs set up a tremendous racket. Comstock commented on it
to his watchmates, and it appeared to make him very nervous.
Finally Comstock picked up a boarding knife and walked to the
bow, feeling its razor-sharp edge. He climbed the barrier that
separated the pigpen from the rest of the ship. The pigs seemed
to recognize an enemy, for the squealing grew louder as he approached. He dropped the knife, cursed, rushed forward,
grabbed one pig by a rear trotter and threw it overboard.

54

Just then First Mate Beetle appeared on deck, a lantern in his hand. He demanded an explanation from Comstock then and there. Comstock told Beetle to mind his own business, then he climbed over the barrier and went back to the waist of the ship, ostensibly to check his helmsman and the compass.

Beetle went to the cabin to report to Captain Worth that the boatsteerer was destroying their provisions. Even Captain Worth could not stomach this outrage and interference in the affairs of the ship. He ordered Comstock to the cabin and dressed him down harshly for the affair. The boatsteerer said nothing, but looked the captain in the eye and kept his thoughts to himself. That attitude set well with Captain Worth, who took it to mean that Samuel Comstock was taking the discipline with good grace. Comstock never gave a hint of anything else, and Worth's friendship for him did not cease.

The whales came—but sparingly; absolutely nothing like the phenomenon of the previous voyage of the *Globe*, during which whale was sighted almost daily. Soon the pigs were gone, and Cook Cleveland began to move farther back in the casks of salted meat. Then came trouble. One cask and then another were found to be spoiled. Whether it was from insufficient salting, or whether the chandlers had cheated them, the meat was foul and inedible and had to be thrown overboard. Some of the crew suggested that the owners and Captain Worth had conspired to line their pockets at the expense of the men—which was most unlikely. The Mitchell company operated several ships and this trouble had never occurred before. Captain Worth had ordered enough meat to provide three barrels a month for the crew for two years—a very generous allowance. Now the ration was cut to less than half that amount, and the men were angry and unhappy. This attitude did not help the whaling; the men were surly and slow, and Captain Worth began to invoke the disciplinary measures for which he was well known.

At the end of another two months off Japan, the *Globe* had aboard less than 300 barrels of oil, a disappointing amount for the time already spent. August brought only another two whales. Now the crew was complaining daily, and Captain Worth was equally annoyed because he believed his men were letting opportunities pass them by.

One summer day one of the men was heard grousing about the food again. Worth rushed forward, grabbed the man by the collar and half choked him. He ordered Cooper Coffin to bring up a handful of iron hoops, then he thrust them at the complainer and the others who stood around. If they did not like the food aboard the ship, they could eat the hoops, he said.

Then came another complaint. Worth was even more violent. Mate Beetle picked up the man by his shirt and dragged him aft. The hands were called and forced to watch Captain Worth gag the man with a pump bolt and tie the bolt in his mouth. Soon that treatment was meted out to several of the men. Ingham was gagged, and so was Seaman Lewis—both of them sailors from Boatsteerer Comstock's watch.

The harsh treatment neither stopped the complaints nor speeded the coming of the whales. It did make the crew miserable. Cooper Hussey and Seamen Lay, Jones and Columbus Worth stuck together more or less and kept their mouths shut. But the others, and particularly Comstock's watch, muttered constantly among themselves about the captain, and talked about jumping ship.

September came, and then October. The food situation remained the same: there was meat but not enough of it. The grumbling increased.

Had the captain been near South America in the "offshore grounds," he would have pulled into port and replenished the meat supply. But there was no place in the wide Pacific that he could do this. The best he could do would be to head back for Hawaii, and there he could perhaps be able to trade for or buy some casks of meat brought "round the Horn." It was unthinkable that he put into hostile Japan.

Samuel Comstock seemed to approve of all the disciplinary

measures the captain took, even though the food of the officers and boatsteerers was no better than that of the men. However, while Comstock appeared to support Captain Worth, he wrote home to his father in an entirely different vein. "You will soon see the bloody flag hoisted on board the *Globe*," he predicted.

Whaling men wrote home often; the letters were passed to other ships homewardbound and might arrive in a few months, a year, or even after the sailor was home from the sea.

No one aboard saw that letter of Comstock's, not even his brother George. No one guessed what was on the boatsteerer's mind. He was waiting, letting this rebellion build and planning for the day he would act. Let those half-crazed seamen of his watch run amok, kill the officers and take charge of the ship. He could control them, then let matters take their own course.

Finally even Captain Worth sensed defeat in these waters. They had only 550 barrels of oil to show for five months' sailing. The crew was almost rebellious. Something must be done.

The matter was brought to a head on the day that Cook Cleveland got drunk again and ruined the evening meal. Captain Worth had him brought aft and thrashed him with a rope's end, then sent him sober and shivering back to his galley with the final word that when they reached Hawaii he would be discharged and left on the beach. That was how the men learned that Captain Worth had given up the fight, and had decided to go back to Hawaii, replenish their supplies and leave their mail. The reason was not really Cleveland's behavior but the signs of scurvy that Captain Worth had begun to detect among the men. The matter of Cleveland was important enough, but it was just one part of the disciplinary problem.

On the return voyage toward Hawaii, Boatsteerer Comstock did not let up on the men of his watch. It was as if he was trying to drive them to a desperate act. George Comstock spent his time with Hussey and Lay, Jones and Worth, who com-

57

forted him. The others of the waist boat watch kept to themselves even more.

The wind was fair for Oahu, and in a few weeks they were nearing the islands again. They pulled into Pearl Harbor and anchored among the other ships in port, not far from a big East Indiaman that was heading for Asiatic waters. Captain Worth sent Cook Cleveland ashore with all his duffle, and then told First Mate Beetle that he would have to spend some time on the beach until he found a man to replace the cook, for it was unthinkable that the ship sail without a cook, and with so small a crew no one could be detailed to the job.

The level of discontent persuaded Captain Worth against granting shore leave to his crew. He did allow contact with the natives and the canoes were alongside the ship day and night this time, girls and men, bringing fruit and other produce of the islands.

It happened the first night: in the laxity of discipline Comstock paid little attention to the men of his watch, or so he said. In the morning he awakened to find that Ingham, Cook, Prass and Lewis were all gone. They had been joined in their desertion by Henman and Jarret. Six men of the *Globe*—one-half the crew of men before the mast—had deserted in one night! It was a disaster.

Comstock pretended to be shocked and concerned, although no one had pressed these men harder than he in the past few months. They had not proved malleable to his wishes, and now they were gone. With this grand show of indignation Comstock reported the missing men to Second Mate Lumbert in the absence of the first mate. The second mate reported to Captain Worth. The captain was furious and ordered a boat so he could go ashore to call on local authorities for assistance in finding his deserters. For until the men were found or replaced, as everybody aboard the *Globe* knew very well, the whaler could not possibly set out again on her voyage.

8

THE
SANDWICH ISLES

WHEN CAPTAIN WORTH went ashore that day following the desertion of his six seamen, he was accompanied by Boatsteerer Comstock because it was his watch that was gone and he had a special responsibility to find them. The captain was dressed in a blue jacket and dark trousers with the cap of his rank on his head. Boatsteerer Comstock was dressed in a bright-red jacket and light trousers, a combination that aroused the interest of the natives, who were not used to seeing white men in such finery. This blaze of color was something the officers and men of the *Globe* had not previously noticed in the boatsteerer. It was as though he had been holding back until this time, and now had some specific matter in mind.

They went to Honolulu and sought the assistance of King Liholiho's ministers. The Hawaiians obliged by sending troops out to the villages nearby to see if they could find the miscreants. They did find a couple of them, captured them and threw them into the fort outside Honolulu, a wooden castle with thick walls standing twelve feet high. It covered an acre and a half of ground down by the seashore. Inside the fort there was housing for the soldiers, a magazine for powder and shot and small ammunition, and a jail. That jail was kept by the soldiers, largely for the foreign element. Its usual occupants were drunken sailors who slept off their carousal and then were returned to their ships.

Comstock found it easy to gain access to the jail, where the prisoners were kept in fetters, since Captain Worth had said that they were deserters and he wanted them returned to the ship. Somehow in the conversation Comstock managed to indicate to the men that he would come back later and help them. Then he left.

Now Comstock began making his own plans. He went from village to village, looking for likely candidates for his ends. The desertion of the six men of the *Globe* was made to order for him; he had hoped that the men might be led to violence, but when they proved incapable of it, he was ready to seek new assistants. One by one he found his men from among the gang of drunken sailors, deserters and beachcombers who frequented the fringes of Honolulu, getting money and food where they could. Before long, he had four men in mind. That was all he would need.

Samuel Comstock then turned to the pleasures of Honolulu. He walked the streets until he found the liquor shops frequented by sailors. In one of these Comstock encountered a group of men from the East Indiaman in the harbor. They began talking, and suddenly Comstock was struck by a new idea: why not take the East Indiaman instead of the whaler? It was a far more useful ship to him, and the prospect of doing violence to Captain Worth, his one friend aboard the *Globe*, did not appeal to Comstock.

Cautiously Comstock began sounding out his new companions of the Indiaman. He spoke of his dream of a South Sea island kingdom, and these sailors were fascinated, as many might be at such a prospect. Comstock had a persuasive way about him, and he could make a man envisage his dream. He could see that there was interest, although on a first meeting he dared not speak that dread word *mutiny*.

With these friends, Comstock roamed the village of Honolulu. Before the day was ended, one of the sailors persuaded Hawaiian acquaintances to give a feast. The white men would bring the rum; the Hawaiians would supply the food, the fire and the girls. The whole group assembled down on the beach.

The whites stood by, observing judiciously, as their Hawaiian friends made preparations for the feast. The islanders picked a flat place on the beach and dug a hole three feet square, about two feet deep. Using driftwood, dried moss and grass, they built a fire in the hole and piled a heap of small stones on top. Someone had gathered a bushel of taro root bulbs, which were put in for steaming along with fish wrapped in palm leaves and several chickens, ducks and a whole pig secured for baking. After the taro roots were steamed, they were washed, peeled and pounded on a flat wooden plate into the paste called poi, which was essential, the East Indiamen said gravely, to the proper Polynesian enjoyment of rum.

All afternoon the preparations went on while the Americans wandered around the settlement, laughing with the girls and watching the young men fish, swim and exhibit feats of strength to amuse them. Needless to say, the missionaries were not in sight.

By nightfall the meal was ready, and the foreigners and the natives gathered around the pit, sitting cross-legged on the ground, rum bottles within easy reach, opened coconuts beside them, and they feasted. As the gaiety increased, the Hawaiians were persuaded to perform a hula. The girls assembled on one side, long grass skirts and naked breasts undulating in unison as they strummed the ukeleles and the men beat out the cadence on their skin drums.

Much later that night Samuel Comstock made his way back to the fort. He had said he would return and now he had. One of the deserters had managed to get his manacles off, and he helped the other. Comstock gave them both money and directions to a village up by the crater above Pearl Harbor, where they would be sheltered from the king's men and the white searching parties.

Then Samuel Comstock was off in the darkness of the night, on his way back to the ship.

The *Globe* had to be reprovisioned. Captain Worth and his officers went among the ships in the harbor, begging for and buying all they could. Slowly they managed to acquire meat to replace the rotten salt beef that had been thrown overboard off Japan. Comstock was as helpful as he could be, and his red coat soon became famous. Among the Hawaiians he himself was infamous, for he teased the bronzed natives who came aboard the *Globe* to trade, bullied them and struck them with the flat of his cutlass. Among the crews of other vessels he was known for his hard drinking and bad temper. They called him "that rascal in the red jacket."

To Captain Worth, it was very important that all the missing seamen be found or replaced. Comstock made quite sure they would not be found, but he did not yet mention the men he was recruiting, for his mind was off on that other dream, his eyes often falling on the East Indiaman not far away from the ship. How much better to trade cloth and furs and metal ingots for power than to try to parlay whale oil into a kingdom.

Comstock went into the cabin one day and told the Captain that he wanted to be paid off there in Honolulu. The stink of whale was not for him, he said. He had a chance to ship out on the East Indiaman alongside, and he wanted Captain Worth to free him so he could take it.

Captain Worth listened with dismay. Already he had lost his cook and six seamen, and here was a vital member of the crew, almost an officer, trying to get away as well. Worth refused to consider Comstock's pleas. Instead he painted a picture of a bright and shining future for Comstock in the whaling trade.

Looking around the captain's little cabin, the brightest ornament of the ship, Samuel B. Comstock set his teeth and without a word spun around and disappeared. There, in one brief interview, the fate of the *Globe* and her captain was settled. Comstock had been denied his wish and now the ship was sentenced.

All that remained to be decided was the time.

9

THE UNHOLY CREW

WEEKS OF SEARCH brought no sign of the six missing whale-
men—Samuel Comstock made sure of that—and finally Captain Worth decided that he had to ship new men if he
was to get back to whaling. He reached that decision with
reluctance, for it was well known among captains that shipping a crew in a foreign clime was risky business. Sailors
found ashore anywhere but in their homeland were usually
abroad for some good reason: desertion, drunkenness or disciplinary problems. Captain Worth could hardly look forward
to getting the salt of the earth with his dredge; he might well
get the dregs.

First Mate Beetle and the captain scoured the villages
for white men who frequented native settlements: the drunks,
beachcombers and deserters down on their luck. From this
group Captain Worth found seven volunteers to join the
whaling ship on her voyage, and they were as unseemly
a gang as had ever jumped ship in a hot port: all beachcombers.

Silas Payne, unshaven and unkempt, was the first of them,
the leader as they came aboard with their duffel. He was tall,
even skinny, with dark complexion and a black stubble of a
beard. The red in his eye was a compound of rum and rebellion. His reputation was so soiled in his native Sag Harbor on
New York's Long Island, that it was said the community had

heaved a collective sigh of relief when he shipped out on a whaler, and an even greater one when it was learned that he had jumped ship in Honolulu.

John Oliver was Payne's close companion; a short, cringing little man from Shields, England, who spoke with a strange gutter accent and was forever making coarse jokes at the expense of his comrades and the world in general. His relations with women had apparently never progressed beyond the whorehouse stage, and his talk about the female sex was almost entirely in terms of organs of reproduction.

Anthony Hanson was a younger man; he had the attribute of at least coming from Barnstable on Cape Cod. He was shipped as cook to replace John Cleveland. And his cooking was good enough; at least as long as the fresh fruit and vegetables and the chickens, ducks and pigs held out, it would be good enough. Once they were gone, then that was the time a ship's cook showed his mettle—the man who could take the basic necessities of life and keep a hungry crew from crying was a real one, and a gem.

Next came Joseph Thomas. He shipped as steward. He was a Connecticut man originally, but not an admirable one. He had been drunk and on the beach here for months. Also in this crew was William Humphreys, a black, who had his own reasons for being on the beach in Hawaii, reasons that had much to do with the place of men of color in a white society. Then came Thomas Liliston, a Virginian who had jumped ship in Hawaii and drunk himself half to death before he ran out of money, credit and friends, in that order.

Last, seventh, was a man the captain put down on the crew list as Joe Brown, because he could not possibly pronounce his native name. Joe Brown was a Hawaiian, the best of a very bad lot, with no experience in sailing on whalers, but some in sailing on American ships. He had immense good will and he was determined to be useful. His employment was a sign of Captain

Worth's desperation; but there simply were not that many men ashore who would sail at any price.

Of the seven men, four were Samuel Comstock's creatures: Silas Payne, John Oliver, Joseph Thomas and Thomas Liliston. The boatsteerer had outlined his plan to them in part. He had stopped with the capture of the ship, the sailing of the *Globe* to a Pacific isle, and the establishment there. He had not, obviously, told them that once he had found the island and burned the ship, the next step was to destroy the men with him. That idea was so monstrous that it never seemed to occur to his fellow conspirators.

Captain Worth, desperate to be gone on his business again, accepted the men for what they were. He signed them and they moved into their quarters, forward. Joe Thomas was first assigned as steward, to oversee the purchase and loading of the last supplies. Almost immediately he and the captain quarreled over food, each accusing the other of trying to cheat the men. Sensing more trouble, Captain Worth appointed the black man, Humphreys, as assistant steward.

The *Globe* sailed off on a Sunday, bound for the waters south and east of Hawaii, where Captain Worth hoped to change the bad luck that had dogged the ship since she set out. Now two years had passed, and Captain Worth had not yet secured a quarter of what he hoped to bring home to Nantucket to guarantee his employment on the next voyage.

The weather was as fine as it could be, and the men, too, had hoped that all the ills of the past were washed away. The ship ran south before a good brisk breeze, her canvas billowing full and staying that way. They were sharp on the lookout for whale. But due south of Hawaii's group they found nothing, although there had been good reports from the area by other ships that came through the islands as Captain Worth had waited there.

Captain Worth consulted his charts and headed north for Fanning Island, which lies just three degrees above the equator. Here, in the past, many a captain had reported success, and in talks with other masters in Hawaii, Worth had heard that the whales were here this year. Even though they were far behind the schedule Worth had set for himself, hope rose anew. Many a captain who had started out with a bad trip had repaired his fortunes in a few weeks.

Although the time was January of this year 1824, and the weather back in Nantucket and Martha's Vineyard was cold and stormy, it could not have been more lovely in these southern waters. The sun was "proud and magnificent," as young George Comstock called it. For a week, or almost a week, it appeared that the voyage was indeed headed for success and pleasure, as a whaling voyage ought to be when the grease was not running. The captain had regained his optimism, the crew had recovered from all signs of scurvy, and their spirits were up. Boatsteerer Comstock had apparently taken well to his new watch, for he was jovial and easy on them, and there was no sign of the old hauteur or harshness.

But at the end of only the fourth day out, the troubles started up again. The men were up, the assignments of the day were set, the crosstrees manned, and breakfast was set for seven o'clock. It was another magnificent sunny day, with a following wind sending them on their way.

Then came the grub, and a short ration of salt pork. Every man noticed it. Every man had something to say.

All that talk, all those promises about securing more meat from other ships in Hawaii—they were lies, the crewmen began telling each other. The grumbling was so immediate and so loud that the mates heard and investigated, and Steward Thomas was summoned to the cabin.

Except in the course of duty, and explicit duty at that, the men did not venture aft of the mizzen, for the vents and skylight of the hatch would have made it possible for the fo'c'sle to know precisely what the cabin was thinking, and this would never do. But this day there was no need for the men to try to eavesdrop. From cabin to waist came the sounds of a violent quarrel between the captain and his new steward.

Each again blamed the other for the rotten meat that had been purchased from these other ships. The *Globe* had been cozened, there was no question about that, but by whom was the matter at issue. The captain, of course, won out by dint of authority. He fired Joe Thomas as steward and sent him forward to serve as a seaman on Boatsteerer Smith's watch.

That was not quite the end of the incident. Joe Thomas went forward, grumbling to the men that Captain Worth had done him and them in. Steward Humphreys tried to explain that they must go on short rations of meat again because the ship had bought foul casks. And the men believed according to their background and nature.

Samuel Comstock said absolutely nothing as Joe Thomas came forward. But later that day Comstock was aloft at the masthead on lookout duty with William Lay. The boatsteerer started a conversation with the young seaman. Here high in the tops no one on deck could hear what was said.

"Well, William," said the boatsteerer as they hung swaying above the ship. "There is bad usage in the ship. What had we better do—run away or take the ship?"

Young Lay was paralyzed with fear at the forbidden thought of mutiny. He had long sensed that there was something brewing behind those cold, strange eyes of Samuel Comstock's and now he shivered to learn what it really was. For the words "take the ship" were uttered so calmly that Lay knew Comstock had considered this idea of mutiny a thousand times so that it no longer shocked the man himself but came out slow and easy.

Lay gave the boatsteerer a half laugh and an evasive answer in order that Comstock would not suspect how frightened he really was, and also so that Comstock would not turn against him. At the end of his watch, Lay tried and tried again to secure a moment's conversation with Second Mate Lumbert, who was his friend among the officers. But whenever Lumbert was in sight, so was Comstock, it seemed, and Lay was terrified lest the boatsteerer discover that he would betray the mutiny. It was apparent that he *did* suspect, for he kept looking at Lay that day with an odd expression on his face, and so intimidated the youth that before the day was out, Lay had given up the idea of telling the second mate. For would he believe? Certainly the captain would not believe—he had more confidence in Comstock than in any other man on the ship, it seemed, even the hard-working Beetle, the honest Lumbert and the open-faced Fisher.

Captain Worth seemed benignly unaware of any difference aboard the ship. But there was a real difference, and it could best be sensed in the forecastle. The boatsteerer's former watchmen, those long gone in the mountains of Oahu, had been secretive among themselves as they planned their escape, but they had never been untoward or unfriendly to the rest of the men in the fo'c'sle. This new batch were birds of a feather, cronies all, and they had nothing to do with the other men. It was most uncomfortable. Of them all only Humphreys, the black, was even decent to the rest.

That same afternoon, after Comstock had approached Lay, the boatsteerer went to the forecastle and there began talking to the men about running away when they reached Fanning Island. He was sounding them out. Lay heard the talk, but no mention of mutiny this time. Still, Lay was more concerned than ever, for Comstock was becoming bold. Something was very wrong in the ship.

Lay sought out Cyrus Hussey, and the two of them tried to get the word aft. But when one wanted to speak to an officer it was surprising how small the ship was and how many men were always watching. Lay and Hussey did not know whom to trust except themselves and the boys Jones and Worth. They could not take the chance of passing a message.

Hussey had no chance at all to inform the officers of the

impending danger. He was confined in the coopers' quarters that afternoon and did not come up.

Lay had one opportunity, or seemed to have. The second mate was in the yards with him, furling the mainsail, and Lay tried to edge over along the yard to give the word. But as if knowing, suddenly Silas Payne was beside them, and the chance was gone.

Still later, Lay and Hussey got together again to exchange further observations about Comstock. A day or two earlier Hussey had seen Comstock pick up a cutlass from the rack in the cabin and take it into his own quarters in the steerage. The boys talked for a long while, and parted fearing the worst was about to happen.

As the night of January 25 fell and the sun slipped below the horizon, the instant blackness of the tropics descended on the *Globe*. A pleasant breeze filled the sails and cooled the men from their day's labors. William Lay, sleeping in the fo'c'sle, was restless and disturbed, and when he awakened from a bad dream, he worried about the next day.

THE
MUTINY

10

"NOW
IS THE TIME . . ."

THE DAWN OF JANUARY 26 broke as suddenly as the night had fallen. The orb of sun pushed its way steadily above the surface of the Pacific to stand redly alone. It promised to be another grand sailor's day, with a flurry of gulls and albatrosses to amuse them, the fleecy clouds drifting overhead, the wind coming strong enough to raise the whitecaps and bring them where they wished to go, but not so strong as even to discommode a sailor.

William Lay arose hurriedly, furled his hammock, stowed it and made his way to the tops. He had no desire for conversation with Boatsteerer Comstock.

George Comstock was sleeping in the forecastle; he awoke to grab his pannikin and his utensils and appear at the galley for his grub. He was totally unaware of events of the past few days. Although Samuel was his brother, he scarcely ever spoke to him except on watch, and then being brother did not seem to help him but instead secured him longer stands at the helm than any other.

George was disturbed by the Thomas incident of a few days before. He did not know what to believe about Captain Worth; he knew that he did not care for Joe Thomas, the dark-faced, evil-smiling man from Connecticut. If there was hanky-panky in the stores, he was inclined to believe it was the steward and not the captain who had been cheating the men.

The captain, as all the hands had observed, had grown nervous in recent days, since the Thomas episode, and he had made as if to flog one of the men, for some relatively unimportant error. The air was charged. It was creating a definite change in the sea manners of the crew. The *Globe* had been queen of the whalers under Captain Gardner, and any man who sailed in her had been proud, even boastful, of his craft and mates. But now they were a gang of hangdogs traveling through the endless Pacific with no apparent purpose. It had been weeks since they had a whale; all they had was trouble and suspicion and unhappiness among them.

This morning at his post in the tops William Lay sensed the tension and redoubled his straining to find a spout. If only they would find whale, all these emotions might quickly pass in the excitement of the chase and the hard, exhausting work of trying out that left man and officer as spent as if they were indeed equal.

The captain came on deck, to make his morning tour. Usually he did not venture all the way forward; today something impelled him to do so, and as he moved up along the ship, smoking his cigar and observing, he noted something that dissatisfied him. He saw that the face brace was loose, and he turned to the seaman standing near it. "Take a pull on the face brace there, my man," he said.

The seaman was Joseph Thomas, lately steward. He heard his captain, but he lounged back against the capstan. The captain stopped.

"I said, 'Sailor, take a pull on the face brace.' If you are not deaf, say 'Aye, aye, sir' before you set to work."

Thomas glowered, turned away from the captain and set out to do the task assigned him.

All the frustrations of the past two years' unsuccessful voyage now seemed to loosen in the captain. He strode forward two steps, grasped Thomas by the shoulder with his left hand, swung him around, cocked his right fist and drove it squarely into the man's jaw, knocking him down. Thomas picked himself off the deck, got to a sitting position and looked up, swearing.

The captain reached for him again, gave him an uppercut that knocked him back onto the deck, and then turned. "Do your work, sailor, or I will knock you to hell. Remember that." The words were flung over his shoulder in a flurry of cigar smoke as Captain Worth went swiftly aft to regain his composure.

"You will pay for it if you do," Thomas shouted, pulling himself up.

Beetle was standing there, First Mate Beetle who had taken so many breaches of discipline from this unruly crew, and particularly from the men of Comstock's watch. He said not a word but moved to Thomas, picked up the man by the scruff of his jacket and smacked him on both sides of the face. Thomas flinched and ran to escape. The mate cursed and caught him, then dragged the seaman back aft to the quarter-deck, where the captain was smoking his cigar.

"He continued to be insolent, sir," said the mate.

"All right," said the captain. "Then it is time the crew had a lesson. Fetch me a rope's end."

The men not actually in the rigging or belowdecks on duty stood in the waist, silent and watchful, as Beetle moved to a locker and secured the item wanted, a two-foot length of manila, two and a half inches in diameter, with a tarred end to keep it from unraveling, the business (or striking) end cunningly held together in splices. Beetle then stripped off Thomas' shirt and held him by the throat, back to the mizzen for bracing, while Captain Worth removed his jacket and proceeded to lay on with a strong right arm. It was a good ten minutes later when the half insensible, bleeding Thomas was pulled to the forecastle and dumped down the companionway into the hands of his mates. A panting Beetle glared but said

73

not a word. Half the men had watched the performance and were staring silently at the mate. As Mr. Beetle went back aft, the muttering began.

"By God, we'll not take this kind of torture" was one remark.

"Revenge it!" came the fierce whisper from Samuel Comstock.

But the men were not thinking of revenge. They were talking escape, and they talked seriously. The place to escape was Fanning Island. They would seize a boat and get away.

That was Thomas and Liliston talking. Thomas went below and the others bathed his bruised back while they continued the discussion.

"We'll take a boat on our watch," Liliston said, "and make for the island. They'll never find us there."

"I say revenge it," Samuel Comstock said again. "They will find you at Fanning, and then it will go the worse."

All the others were silent except Rowland Jones, the young boy who had always been a favorite of the captain. "How can you bear to see a man flogged that way!" he shrieked and ran back into the forecastle in his agony.

Gilbert Smith, the second boatsteerer, came to the forecastle to see what he could do for the injured Thomas. Almost for the first time during the voyage, Smith was making his presence felt among his fellows. For although he and Comstock shared the boatsteerers' quarters forward in the steerage, they had virtually no contact. Smith was repelled by Comstock's rough seaman's habits, his drinking and his womanizing. Smith was a very religious young man, and in fact was the unofficial chaplain of the ship. He never joined a yarnfest or a singing bout. He did not drink or smoke, and he was clean-shaven. He did his duty, and so far he had left a slight mark on the ship.

This visit to succor the wounded Thomas was the first indication on the voyage that Smith was really human, that he ever stepped beyond the bounds of duty. But Comstock, in-

74

stead of welcoming the new recruit to the band of conspirators, turned on him.

"What are you doing down here, you spy?" he demanded.

Smith glanced at him querulously. What had he done to be called spy?

"Yes, I said 'spy,'" Comstock reiterated. "By God, now you've done it. You've heard our talk and we'll not let you live. You had best be sure we are gone tonight and that you keep your lip buttoned. Otherwise you'll not live to see the sun rise."

Comstock was sitting on Thomas' sea chest at the end of the bunk row. He made as if to rise right then and carry out his threat with the knife in his belt.

At this moment, from the masttop came the hail: "Sail ho! A ship, two points off the larboard bow. She looks a whaler."

The coming of that sail suspended all activity. No desertion, no mutiny, if that was to be the end, could possibly be carried out in the presence of another ship. They might sail in consort, they might find all the whale that anyone wanted. In any event, they were no longer on the sea alone, and the circumstances that had guided the men this morning were already completely changed.

The forecastle emptied. Even Joe Thomas slowly donned his shirt, pulling it painfully over his back, and then trudged up the companionway to stand at the rail and peer at the oncoming ship.

She was the whaler *Lyra* out of New Bedford, Captain Joy commanding, and it so happened that the captain and Worth knew each other. So it was time for a gam. The first and second mates went over to the other ship. So did Boatsteerer Comstock. He suddenly professed great concern for the way in which this other vessel worked, and insisted that he be taken. His arguments were sound enough to Captain Worth, so he was detailed to go. Meanwhile Captain Joy and one of his mates came aboard the *Globe,* and the two captains brought out a bottle of Worth's best brandy and began talking about the difficulties of finding whale this season. The *Lyra* was apparently in much the same situation as the *Globe,* and as the bottle diminished and the day wore on, the two captains decided to act together for a time. They would sail together, and would put up lights to show any change in course that might occur during the night-time hours.

Being in agreement, the two captains spent a pleasant day. Aboard the *Lyra,* however, matters were going a bit differently. When the mate of that vessel asked Mr. Beetle how life progressed on his ship, Beetle looked straight at Boatsteerer Comstock before replying, and while speaking to the other mate, he never took his eyes off the boatsteerer. They had one bad troublemaker aboard, Beetle said loudly. And the real problem was that he seemed to have the ear of the captain.

The mate of the *Lyra* had already enjoyed a rum or two, and the interplay was lost on him. He launched into a long tale of another whaler where a Jonah had been shipped by an indulgent captain and had caused the wreck of the ship and the loss of half its men before the old man realized how wrong he had been.

But Comstock glared at Beetle with the most insolent look of which he was capable, and then swaggered down the deck to confer with his counterparts, looking back only once.

When Comstock returned from his sojourn aboard the *Lyra* he had recovered all geniality. He saw Smith on deck, just before Smith was to take the watch, and he gave no sign of his previous deadly intent but passed a pleasant enough greeting to the other boatsteerer.

The *Lyra*'s boat that brought back Comstock and the mates waited then for their captain to finish his gam with Captain Worth, and the men settled down on deck to take it easy. Playing host, Samuel Comstock remained with his new acquaintances, making small talk or splicing the foresheet. As they talked they watched the sun go down, always a sight to impress a man in that climate.

Comstock looked up and gazed at the horizon. "That sight reminds me of the saying of a Roman general on the eve of a battle: 'How many that watch that sun go down will never see it rise again.' "

His listeners looked respectfully at a man of the sea who possessed so much erudition. But being unaware of the morning's events and those that had gone before, the sailors from the *Lyra* were in no position to realize the significance of Boatsteerer Comstock's present thinking. It was just another remark to them.

Captain Joy returned to his vessel shortly after darkness came, and then the watches were set.

First Mate Beetle appeared on deck to inform Boatsteerer Smith of the order for the night. They would sail along on the present course until twelve o'clock midnight. At that point, the wind permitting, they would change course and then hold that tack for the rest of the night, moving into waters where the two captains adjudged there was a good chance of finding whale. As they tacked, the boatsteerer would send one man into the foretop with a lighted lantern to show the *Lyra* that they had moved as directed.

So the first watch was set. Smith's watch ran from dark until ten o'clock, when Comstock's waist-boat watch would take over. Comstock would then be on watch until two in the morning, when Third Mate Fisher and his boat crew would take over until dawn. There seemed to be a certain inequity; sometimes Smith's watch lasted only three hours, and so did that of Fisher, but on the other hand, depending on where the ship might lie, sometimes their watches lasted five hours, while Comstock's was always four.

After Beetle had set the watch, the sails were reefed down and Smith was in charge of the ship, with plenty of time for meditating. Captain Worth appeared on deck at eight o'clock, smoking his after-dinner cigar. He gazed around him, and in a quiet voice ordered another reef taken in the topsails, and changed the orders. The watch was to keep the ship by the wind until two o'clock, then tack if the wind was right and set the signal for the *Lyra*.

Just before ten o'clock the rouster awakened Samuel Comstock and the other members of the waist-boat watch. They yawned and stretched and made their various ways to the deck, to stand by the helm while Boatsteerer Smith gravely passed on the orders of the night. "You take the helm, George," Comstock said. "And hold her a good full." He then went off to set the other men at their tasks while George Comstock settled down to steer the ship for the next two hours. When his time for relief had come he would pick up the rattle, a large gourd filled with beans which made a noise that could be heard anywhere on deck, and he would signal that it was time for his relief.

They were moving through patches of thick mist that made it impossible for young George Comstock to see anything farther than his binnacle and to catch an occasional glimpse of the headsails. Behind, once in a while he could see the lights of the *Lyra* as she followed faithfully in the *Globe*'s path, but when the *Lyra* entered the mist they were blotted out, reappeared and were blotted out again, until he grew used to keeping track of position by rapid glances.

Fifteen minutes went by, then half an hour. He steered on. Then he heard voices in the waist, voices of people whispering quietly but rapidly together. There were two, no more, and they grew excited. One voice was raised, and then came another—he was sure it was his brother's—shouting the man down.

George Comstock tried to hear what was said. But he could make out nothing but talk in rapid tones, too muffled for deciphering.

Another fifteen minutes passed, and then there was quiet. He steered on, watching his sails lest they luff, and making sure to keep a point off the wind so the square rigger would draw.

Suddenly he felt a presence behind him. "Well," came a voice which he recognized as Sam's. "What are you up to?"

George said nothing but gave a helpless gesture to indicate that he was doing what he should be, steering the ship.

"Keep the ship a good full, I told you," Samuel Comstock said fiercely.

George looked at his compass. He was right on course, a point off the wind.

"You're letting her slip. I saw the headsails shaking."

George had caught a glimpse of the headsails even as his brother came up silently behind him, and they were drawing well. He knew suddenly that his brother was lying about the sails. But why?

"I'm right on the point," he protested. He was not ready then for Samuel's next gesture. The boatsteerer wrested the helm from his brother's hands, and put it up so the ship ran out a full two points off the wind, then thrust the wheel back at George.

"Mind what I tell you," he said with a fierceness George had never heard in his voice before. And then Samuel left the helm and went forward again.

Looking behind, George suddenly realized precisely what his brother had done, and why. The *Lyra,* when next he spotted her through the mist, was steadily moving away from them on the course they had been following. The light grew perceptibly smaller as he watched.

So that was it. To lose track of the *Lyra.* But for what reason?

Below him in the waist, the sound of whispering resumed. Several more times in the next half-hour Samuel Comstock came to the helm again to see that George was steering at least two points off the wind, and each time he left he went back to the waist, and the whispering started up again.

Then the whispering stopped. To George it was worse than if it had continued. He was thoroughly frightened and ready for anything when he heard his brother speak in a low voice.

"Now is the time," he said.

11

MURDER AT MIDNIGHT

In the silence of the night George Comstock watched the hourglass run out, which meant it was twelve o'clock midnight and time for him to be relieved of the helm. The quartermaster's work was most arduous, for he must keep alert and keep the ship's bow pointing on course regardless of the change in breezes or the seas that tried to trick him. He had put in his two hours; now it was time for Samuel to assign another to the task.

George picked up the rattle and gave it one shake. Immediately his hand was seized in a viselike grip from behind, and the rattle was silent.

"Stop that racket," hissed Samuel Comstock, whose hand held his brother's tightly.

"It's not my helm and I want to be relieved." George said.

His brother turned on him again. "If you make the least damn bit of noise," he said, "I will send you to hell." Samuel put the rattle down carefully on the deck, then moved away, first stopping to be certain that his warning had been appreciated by George, who was so frightened that all he could do was watch the binnacle, keep the ship pointed two points off the wind and pray. The ship luffed, and panic seized him. Furiously he swung the wheel to get those sails to drawing again lest the captain sense the change and come on deck, or his brother come back and murder him as he had promised.

There was no question in George's mind but that there was dark work afoot somehow. He did not know what the whispering was about, but he knew it was menacing. And he sensed that his brother had gone mad. The idea of securing help came to him, and he lifted the rattle again. But at its first sound Samuel Comstock appeared, and for the third time threatened George.

Samuel Comstock lit a lantern and went down into the steerage, where the whaling tools of the trade were kept, the spades and knives and hooks needed to separate the blubber from the flesh. George trembled. He thought of home, and how little chance there was that he would ever see his father or his other brothers and sisters again. They would never know that he had been murdered by his very own brother. The events quite overcame the teenage boy, and silent sobs shook his shoulders as he stood glued to the wheel, waiting for sounds that must bring disaster.

Then George heard a shuffling noise, and his brother appeared at the helm once again. He came up to the work bench next to the helm and laid down something heavy. That was all. No words passed between them. Samuel disappeared into the cabin gangway, and George again picked up the rattle as if to summon help. But his courage left him. "I dare not," he said. "He will kill me sure." He put the rattle back down on the deck. He looked at the compass and tested the wind, holding the wheel steady.

Samuel came back and picked up what he had left. Behind trailed Silas Payne, John Oliver, William Humphreys and Thomas Liliston. When they actually opened the hatch, Liliston hung back. They had been talking all night about what they were going to do, and Liliston had been as brave and ready as any of the rest. But when it came to action, he reconsidered at the last moment and dropped behind, and instead of passing down the gangway, he retraced his steps across the waist to the fo'c'sle hatch, tumbled down as fast as his legs would carry him, and in a moment was in his bunk.

From George Comstock's vantage point, there was absolute silence now. He could see nothing but the lights of the *Lyra,* now dim specks, as she moved steadily on a diverging course, thinking all the while that she was in the trail of the *Globe* and would be signaled when the other tacked.

Not a sound. The wind rustled through the rigging. The flicker of the sails was sensed more than seen in the darkness as the wind played little tricks around the luff. George stood, still paralyzed, half knowing what must be going on, and waiting.

Then he heard a blow.

Down below, Samuel Comstock moved steadily by the dim glow of the lantern he carried. The instrument he had laid down on the workbench was a deadly boarding knife, with its long handle and double-sharpened four-foot blade, two inches wide. He entered the cabin and prepared to make for the captain's stateroom on the starboard side, aft. But it was a hot night in these latitudes, and the wind was from the port quarter, which meant that the captain's quarters were getting very little air. For this reason the captain had deserted his stateroom and lay slumbering on his back in his hammock tied up in one end of the cabin.

The knife seemed too large for these close quarters. Comstock put it down, then picked up an ax. Comstock raised the lantern high with his left hand and gazed down on the calm face of the sleeping man, who had befriended him so many times. He gave no time for thought—the captain had sealed his death warrant with the refusal to let Comstock ship on the East Indiaman back in Honolulu harbor. He raised the ax high, and with one powerful blow of his strong right arm he brought it down on the top of Captain Worth's head.

The captain groaned but made no other noise. His skull

was smashed, and the top of his head nearly cut off. The arm came back, the ax descended once again, and Captain Worth was dead, blood dripping down from the hammock onto the deck of the cabin.

Comstock ran back to where Payne was waiting while the boatsteerer struck the telling blow. "Quick," he shouted, "get the mate!"

Payne now had the deadly boarding knife. He opened the mate's cabin door on the port side of the vessel and made a thrust at Beetle. The light of the lantern near Comstock and Payne showed their faces as they approached. Payne made a second thrust with the boarding knife but missed.

Now Beetle awakened and saw them. "What . . . what . . . what . . . ?" he exclaimed in disbelief. "Is this . . . Oh, Payne, oh, Comstock! Don't kill me, don't! Have I not always . . ." The mate's voice trailed off as Payne again struck him with the big boarding knife that was much too clumsy for the task. It bent.

Now Comstock stepped forward. Recognized, and with the captain murdered behind him, there was nothing to lose by talk, nothing to gain by dissembling. "Yes," he shouted, purple with rage. "You have always been a damn rascal. You tell lies of me out of the ship, will you? It's a damn good time to beg now, but you're too late." He signed to Payne to kill the man.

This little scene had given Beetle a chance to gather his sleepy senses about him. He sprang from the berth and seized Comstock by the throat. The mate was a big man, taller and stronger than Comstock, and he got enough of a grip to force the boatsteerer to drop his lantern on the deck and fight with both hands to save himself from strangulation.

The lamp glass shattered on the deck and the light went out. When Comstock dropped his ax, Beetle moved, for the first time having a sense of hope that all was not lost.

"Payne, Payne!" Comstock shouted, his voice muffled as the

mate sought a death grip. "He's choking me. The ax, the ax! I dropped it."

Payne released his hold on the boarding knife and fumbled for the ax in the blackness of the little cabin. The very smallness of the quarters helped him; there were only a few feet of space onto which it could have fallen. He found the ax, grasped it by the handle, moved over to the struggling men and pressed it into Comstock's hand.

Breathing heavily, still struggling with one hand to keep the mate's relentless fingers from his throat, Comstock managed to swing the ax and struck the mate a glancing blow in the temple which fractured his skull, knocked him loose from Comstock's throat and sent him to the floor, where he lay, then got up and fell into the pantry to collapse again, writhing in pain.

Comstock passed the lantern to William Humphreys, who got it lit again despite the shattered glass and came back to shine it down on the groaning mate. Little Oliver, now with the boarding knife, danced around to poke at the mate, yet be sure he was not grasped by a hand that could pull him down. Comstock stepped forward impatiently and with another hard swing of the ax nearly decapitated the mate.

The cabin was now a sea of carnage: the captain lay dead in his hammock, blood and brains dripping down. A few feet away the blood-soaked body of First Mate Beetle lay sprawled, half in the pantry. One of Silas Payne's blows at the mate had bent the boarding knife near double and gashed across the mate's ribs and abdomen, cutting a vein and letting a prodigious amount of blood loose. It seemed they were scupper-deep in gore.

The two other miscreants, Oliver and Humphreys, stood guard outside the latched cabin of the other mates. Comstock hesitated but for a moment, decided he needed more light, so he picked up a new lantern, then moved up the passageway, heading for the binnacle.

Thus far the plan had succeeded admirably. It called for Comstock to dispatch the captain, Payne to kill the mate, and the other conspirators to stand guard outside the cabin shared by the second and third mates and kill them with bayonets if they so much as stirred.

The noise in the cabin aroused Boatsteerer Smith, who was sleeping without clothes in his bunk in the steerage. He jumped out of his berth and ran aft, through the waist to the deck, where he knew the helmsman would be. Passing by the companionway that led to the cabin, he looked down, and by the light of Humphreys' lantern he saw the terrible sight below. The mate's neck was propped on the coaming of the pantry, the head lolling with the movement of the ship as though the man were still conscious, just turning his head. The postures of Payne and Humphreys indicated that they were on guard against something. Little Oliver danced around, grinning in his glee. And Comstock, broken lantern in hand, was heading toward the companionway, his shirt covered with blood.

Smith darted to the helm and made his presence known to George Comstock with a silent plea that he not be betrayed. Then he raced into the steerage, dressed and went to the fo'c'sle. Here was his chance to avenge the mutiny. He saw part of what had happened and guessed the rest, and he knew there were only four mutineers to all the rest of them. They could arm themselves with boarding knives, spades and lances from the steerage, and they could take the ship in a few minutes. But they needed a leader, and in this moment of decision, Gilbert Smith's courage failed him. He recalled what he had seen, the look of Comstock, and he collapsed.

Samuel Comstock was indeed a dreadful sight as he emerged from the cabin. The blows against the captain, in which he had raised the ax to the carling over the transom, had left all Comstock's upper body smeared with blood and brain. The severed blood vessels of Beetle's body had splashed the shirt of the boatsteerer and made him as terrible a sight as any officer slaving at the try-pots had ever been. His hair was wild and unkempt and his eyes flamed with fury—this was the sight that met the horrified gaze of the sensitive, religious Smith before he recoiled and ducked back into the shadows.

George Comstock had seen Smith, all right, but he did not betray the other boatsteerer as his brother charged from the gangway. Instead he ventured a cautious question. "Smith? What will you do about him? Do you mean him harm?"

"Yes, I will kill him! Where is he?"

"I haven't seen him," George lied, for Smith was so close upon them, in the shadows, that a hand reached out would touch his leg.

George suddenly turned his back to his brother, and his shoulders began to shake.

"What the hell are you crying about?" the elder Comstock demanded.

"I'm afraid you will hurt me."

Comstock looked the utter disgust he felt. "I will if you do not be quiet!" he shouted.

Reaching over the binnacle, Samuel Comstock then lit his lantern with a steady hand and went back to his bloody business below, casting one hard glance at his brother, who was standing at the wheel trying to pull himself together.

The moment the elder Comstock's back disappeared down the gangway, Smith was in motion. He rushed across the waist and into the fo'c'sle, where he assembled the seamen—everyone had been awakened by the mate's shout and groans. "Comstock's going to kill me," he said to the others, not in fright, but in wonderment as if it were impossible that his life could have come to this. "What shall I do?"

"Go aloft and stay there," one of the seamen said. "By the time he looks for you he may have cooled off."

"Hide in the chain locker," said another.

But Smith, considering his alternatives, did nothing at all, but sat down on a sea chest in the fo'c'sle and awaited events. The Lord would bring whatever end he had in mind for the Christian boatsteerer.

At the helm a shaking George Comstock listened and heard every word of what now happened down in the cabin and the adjoining stateroom of the second and third mates.

Samuel Comstock had stopped in the cabin, reached into the case where the ship's weapons were kept and drawn forth a pair of muskets. These guns were used to shoot sharks, to repel unfriendly natives and for the general defense of the ship. There were bayonets to fit them, and Comstock attached one bayonet to each musket, then loaded the guns.

Oliver and Humphreys were standing guard over the door of the cabin where the two other mates slept. But the mates were not sleeping; they huddled in their bunks, not knowing what had happened, except that the captain and the mate had been at least wounded by the mutineers. But who were they and how many? Comstock was the only one who had spoken aloud, when he shouted at First Mate Beetle, but his voice was so distorted by rage that the mates could not be sure it was indeed he.

Payne was supposed to kill these others, but he stood thunderstruck in the cabin, regarding the carnage they had wrought. Comstock moved on relentlessly by himself. He had long since toured the ship to have a lay of the cabin and the officers' staterooms, and he had a good idea of how Lumbert and Fisher would be arranged in their bunks. He moved up next to the door and fired one of the muskets through. There was no sound from inside. Then he raised his voice and asked, "Are either of you shot?"

Mate Fisher replied hollowly, "Yes, I am shot in the mouth." The ball had passed through one of his cheeks, knocked out some teeth and passed out the other side. The injury was painful but not nearly fatal.

"What are you going to do?" Second Mate Lumbert demanded. "Are you going to kill me, too?"

Comstock replied airily, "Oh, I guess not."

The remark indicated that the mates had a chance for life. Second Mate Lumbert opened the door of the tiny cabin, so they might bargain for it. Comstock had the temerity to grin at him and laugh as though they were sharing some private joke.

But then, in a flash, Comstock lashed out at the second mate with a bayonet. He missed the blow, Lumbert dodged aside and Comstock fell on the deck. In a moment Lumbert had him by the throat, but Comstock got to his knees. He had dropped the musket and bayonet, and they skittered across the floor. Fisher made a dive for them and picked them up. Outside stood Payne and Humphreys and Oliver, but the tiny stateroom was so small that they could not get inside to help their companion.

As Comstock stood up, Fisher had his chance. He held the gun and bayonet, and they were aimed at the boatsteerer's heart. At that moment Fisher had the whole mutiny in his control, had he been given the perspicacity to thrust, and kill the chief mutineer.

Lumbert watched dumbly. Fisher stood there, blood dripping from his broken mouth, and with the bayonet pointed squarely at the boatsteerer's heart. Would he thrust it home and take his chances?

Comstock looked at Fisher severely, playing the role of captain. "Don't you move that an inch!" he said quietly.

Fisher hesitated when he might have struck.

"Put down the gun," Comstock said.

Fisher looked at him, and it was apparent that he was weakening. He did not know how many mutineers were behind the boatsteerer. He calculated, and in his calculation he lost. He put down the gun. Immediately Comstock grabbed it, turned and ran it through Lumbert three times.

Lumbert collapsed on the floor. "Oh, Comstock," he cried, more in sorrow than hurt, "I've a poor old father with six little children at home!"

Comstock sneered and kicked the injured man. "Damn you, so have I."

He then turned to Fisher as Lumbert wriggled and grasped his torn abdomen with both hands. "You," he said. "There is no hope for *you*."

When Fisher looked uncomprehending, Comstock answered the silent question. "You'll remember the *Enterprise,* and my promise?"

Fisher nodded dumbly. He remembered only too well. "But that was weeks ago, and I had no desire to quarrel with you, you remember that?"

"No matter, you made a fool of me before the world. And for that you will die. You have got to die, and you may as well die like a man."

Fisher did more. He turned his back on the boatsteerer. "If that's the way it is," the big third mate said, "and there is no hope, I can see. I will die like a man. I am ready."

Comstock detached the bayonet. Then he put the muzzle of the piece to Fisher's head, and without a qualm pulled the trigger. The third mate's body gave a convulsive jerk, the bone and blood and brains spattered the bulkhead with a nasty greasy stain. The slack body slumped to the floor in an awkward position, as though someone had just let the stuffing out of a tall scarecrow.

Comstock stepped back, his bloody work done for the moment. Now all that remained to be dealt with were the other boatsteerer and the remainder of the crew.

But as he stepped across Lumbert's body, the mate spoke up again in a voice scarcely louder than a whisper. "Spare me, Comstock, spare my life."

Comstock looked down at him, furious. "I am a bloody man," he boasted. "I have a bloody hand and I'll be damned if you will live." He stepped across to the door, and ran the second mate through with his bayonet.

Lumbert groaned. "At least for God's sake, give me some water!"

"I'll give you water," Comstock shouted, enraged because Lumbert refused to die. He reached back and with all his force plunged the bayonet again to the hilt into Lumbert's body, pulled it out, wiped it and walked out the door into the cabin.

George Comstock saw a man coming up the companionway, but it was no one he had ever seen before. Samuel Comstock's eyes were glassy, his mouth hung half loose as though he were drunk on blood, and he moved swiftly, jerkily as he came up. He paid not the slightest attention to George but hastened forward, muttering to himself, and along behind him followed Payne, Oliver and Humphreys, the first two pale and silent, and Humphreys shaking his head slowly.

12

AND WHO SHALL
DIE NEXT?

SAMUEL COMSTOCK passed through the waist. He stopped for a moment to consider whether or not to descend into the steerage, then decided against it, concluding that his quarry lay forward of the mast. "Smith," he shouted. "Gilbert Smith! I want you."

In the forecastle Smith and the others listened with terror, for not a man now had the slightest doubt of what had been happening down in the cabin, and no man in the forecastle knew what the mutineers planned next.

Smith, who had been communing with his God these last few minutes, seemed to be the calmest man in the fo'c'sle. He arose at the sound of his name, quietly moved aft to the gangway and ascended to the deck, to meet Comstock halfway along toward the waist as the boatsteerer came searching for him. Comstock still had the musket in his hand.

If Smith flinched, it was inward, for he showed no fear but met the other boatsteerer on his ground. Comstock put aside the weapon and flung his bloody arm about the other's neck in a rude embrace. "You are going to be one of us, are you not?" he demanded.

Smith took a deep breath. "Oh, yes," he lied, "I will do anything you wish."

It was the right answer, and it saved Boatsteerer Smith's life at that moment. But beneath this sudden change of mind by the bloody Comstock there was reason for sparing the other boatsteerer. For Comstock, although a Godless man himself, believed thoroughly in the reality of hell. Long since he had consigned his own soul to the fire, had sold out willingly for the pleasures of the flesh. But that did not mean he rejected Smith's God entirely. It was not his God, but it was Smith's, and that God should be able to help him. Later he was to tell this to George in a lighter moment, when George puzzled as to why his brother had first asked for the presence of Smith, firmly intending to kill him, and had then turned around and greeted the pious boatsteerer as a long-lost brother met on the shores of a promised land.

The confrontation of Comstock with Smith settled the problem of authority: with the captain and all three mates dead, Comstock and the little band of mutineers were in control of the ship. Comstock held a gun, his associates were all armed, and save for their working knives, not one of the seamen in the forecastle had a weapon at hand. Nor would they have them, for even as Comstock stood, embracing Smith, the henchmen were heading back to the cabin to secure the weapons and make the ship safe for mutiny.

Comstock's next action was to prove he was captain. "All hands on deck," he shouted briskly, and when the men assembled beneath the foremast, he lined them up and sent them into the futtocks to make all sail the ship would carry. Nor did he forget for a moment the nearness of the *Lyra,* which had been falling off on the port quarter all that evening since he issued the fateful orders to his younger brother.

Up into the tops went a seaman carrying the lantern that was the signal for the *Lyra* to tack. Of course, the *Globe* tacked not at all, but Comstock returned to the fearful George and told him to start steering on the wind to make all headway possible.

John Oliver came forward and again ordered all hands on deck to make sail. Stephen Kidder was sent up onto the fore-topsail yard to let out the reef. His brother Peter was sent to the bow to let go the flying jib. Joe Thomas was on the main yard, loosening the main-topsail. Gilbert Smith was sent first to set the fore-topgallant sail, and when he had done that, Comstock looked at him levelly and sent him aft to set the spanker—as if he were trying out Smith just to see if he would challenge Comstock's authority. But no, Smith was as thoroughly cowed as the next man by the course of events, and he went willingly to work.

Above, the topgallants swept out to fill, and the reefs shook out of the big sails. Two men finally had to set the flying jib, and the *Globe* heeled in the fresh breeze as she picked up speed and fled in the reach across the wind, as if the mutineers could not wait to be gone from the scene of their bloody action. As the ship began to surge, Comstock swept the deck with a glance, and finding no signs of opposition, headed back down to the carnage in the cabin.

While Comstock was up on deck, his mates had wreaked their private revenge on Captain Worth, paying the body back for all the supposed indignities heaped upon these sailors over the months of their voyage. They ran a boarding knife up through the rectum to transfix the body, the point of the blade coming straight through longitudinally, and when the knife was stymied at the rib cage, they drove it upward with an ax until it emerged from the mouth.

Whatever Comstock thought of this indignity to the man who had been his best friend aboard the ship, he said nothing. For such was the way of mutineers: Comstock might be chief mutineer, but the veil of authority through which he ruled was so thin that he dared not stretch it save on matters of gravest importance. He might be the greatest scoundrel among them, and the man who had driven home the weapon in every case, but they would all hang with him if it came to that, and so the desperation of his companions matched his own, and they were willing to kill again, having been taught by Comstock's hand how easy it could be.

Captain Worth was taken out of the cabin, hammock and all, and rudely dumped over the transom window. Beetle's body was still alive, although those dreadful blows had destroyed his senses and the man never regained consciousness. But dead or alive, he was hauled to the window and thrust out, to splash into the sea, and then rise again, and sink behind the ship.

Comstock helped with this, then tired and gave orders to his henchmen, Humphreys and Oliver and Payne, to bring the bodies of the other two mates on deck. It was a good idea to let the other crewmen have a taste of what was in store for any who might try to mutiny on Captain Comstock's ship.

The mutineers fastened a rope to Third Mate Fisher's neck and dragged the limp corpse up the companionway stairs out onto the waist deck, where it lay, head flopped to one side, arms akimbo, and legs straight out.

They went back down and tied a rope to Second Mate Lumbert's ankles and hauled the body up the stairs, head bumping audibly on every step. The body was pulled to within a few feet of Fisher's, and the men were called down from the mastheads and from their duty to witness.

Comstock supervised as the lesson was given. First Fisher's body was shoved overboard; it bounced on the crest of a wave, then caught in the water, and sank, its rope trailing behind. Lumbert was next. He, too, was still alive, in spite of the five terrible wounds in his belly, and the smashing of his head on the ride up the stairs. As his body was dragged by the feet toward the starboard rail, Lumbert opened his eyes and stared reproachfully up at Samuel Comstock. "You said you would save me," he gasped.

The show had been staged to indicate to the men the omnipotence and glory of the chief mutineer, and instead he was being reproached by a dead body for not having carried out his mission. Comstock turned red with fury and kicked at the body. "I will save you," he shouted. "Haul away, boys." And the other mutineers hauled on the rope and sent Lumbert's body careening over the side.

The mate's strong fingers grasped the plank sheer and held on with the tenacity of life. Comstock walked over to the edge of the deck. "Get an ax and cut off these hands!" he cried. Then he stamped on the fingers, grinding his foot until Lumbert lost his hold and fell into the sea. Even then Lumbert would not give up. The body went down, then reappeared, and Lumbert began to swim, slowly, painfully, after the ship.

Comstock shouted, "Lower a boat. Take the starboard watch. Be quick about it!"

The frightened men of Boatsteerer Smith's watch made ready to launch their craft. But then Comstock reconsidered this problem. He could send Smith and the others, but where would they end up? Would they indeed come back to the ship or would they rescue the mate and head for the *Lyra?* The devil knew that if that were the case, only too soon all the power of the American fleet would be against the *Globe,* for mutiny was the crime unpardonable, and the whole might of a nation could be turned against them.

He shouted again in a moment. "Belay that order and finish making sail. Let him swim for it. Davy Jones will welcome him soon enough."

And so the *Globe* sailed on through the night, the dim hand of Second Mate Lumbert seen clutching upward in a swimming stroke as the men lost sight of him in the whitecaps, and they were alone with their consciences on the wide Pacific.

13

CRIME
AND PUNISHMENT

As if to encourage Samuel Comstock and his bloody band of mutineers, the wind sprang up while they finished their grisly job on deck, and by four o'clock in the morning, before the dawn broke, a fresh breeze was pushing them along at a fast clip. The breeze, and the relief of seeing the end of bloodshed, caused all the members of the crew to turn to with a good will to bring the ship to rights. The mutineers went below to clear the cabin of its mess. They impressed their more peaceful companions to swab the deck and scrape the third mate's brains off the outer bulkhead of the little cabin. Everything that had any connection with the murders was taken from the cabin and cleaned and washed or thrown over the side.

Immediately after the mutineers took over the cabin and Comstock appointed himself captain of the ship, Silas Payne became first mate. Oliver styled himself second mate, and Humphreys was advanced from steward to purser, while George Comstock was appointed steward and put in charge of serving the meals in the cabin to the new officers. Humphreys went through the captain's sea chest when no one else was looking and abstracted a fine silver watch and sixteen dollars in coins. He never did find the captain's real money store.

The mutiny brought Samuel Comstock's mind to thoughts

of piety. One of his first acts was to appoint Gilbert Smith as
the ship's chaplain. That day Smith conducted memorial
services for the dead captain and the other officers. When
George Comstock took courage in hand and asked his brother
why Smith was saved from the fate of all the other officers, Captain Comstock replied that Smith would bring them luck. Had
they killed so religious a man, his God would have turned
against them. By saving him and letting him conduct services
to that God, they were putting Him on their side and would
prosper because of it.

All that Comstock had taught himself now came into play.
He began shooting the sun with the captain's instruments, and
keeping up the log. On January 26 at noon he found their position to be 5°50′ north by 159°13′ west.

He made sure that all the mutineers and the others saw him
shooting the sun. Thus they recognized the one real point of
superiority he had: Comstock was the only man left aboard
the ship who could navigate, so no matter what happened, his
safety was assured as long as they were at sea.

On January 27, the second day after the carnage, the mutineers were employed at cleaning the small arms—fifteen muskets
and a number of pistols, cutlasses, sabers and knives; and in
making cartridge boxes. Captain Comstock also set up a
course of instruction so that every mutineer would be able to
use a firearm if necessary. For he intended to sail to the Pacific islands, and he did not know what they were going to encounter before they found the one marvelous isle of his
dreams. His men would have to protect him.

That day the wind died down and the *Globe* was seized by
a flat calm. The ship lay dead in the water, her unfurled sails
hanging slack. Not even a sea bird moved on the glassy surface
of the water. The heat came to remind them of the torments
of the hell that Samuel Comstock spoke of so often these
days. He was driven from the captain's stateroom into the
cabin, where he hung a hammock, just as Thomas Worth had

hung one before him. The day was bad enough, the heat oppressive, the mutineer's thoughts eating at them with the tenacity of maggots. But the night was far worse.

Before the next day dawned, trouble came. Steward George Comstock, checking the cabin stores in the steerage, as was his duty, came upon his superior, William Humphreys, the purser, loading a pistol.

"What are you doing?" Comstock asked.

"I heard something and I'm going to be ready," Humphreys replied, cutting off the conversation and putting the loaded pistol down beside him.

George Comstock did not know what to do, but blood was still thicker than water. Besides, he was more afraid of his brother than he was of the black or of any of the other mutineers. So George went to Samuel that night and Samuel consulted with Mate Payne, and the two of them asked Humphreys what was on his mind.

"I'm afraid," the black man said.

"Afraid of what?" Comstock demanded.

"Afraid for my life."

"Nonsense!" Comstock shouted. "You come and see me before you do any more loading of pistols. Now you tell me just what makes you afraid for your life."

Thereupon Humphreys told how he had heard Gilbert Smith and Peter Kidder talking about retaking the ship. He was afraid they would do so and kill all the mutineers. That was why he had gotten the pistol and loaded it.

The story seemed thin to Samuel Comstock. Peter Kidder was notable among the crew for his shyness. "It is senseless. Kidder is too easily scared," Comstock told Silas Payne. "There is more to the story than this."

There was also more to Comstock's rejection of the Humphreys story than appeared on the surface: the mutineers had been falling out almost as soon as they began their dreadful course.

Comstock trusted none of them. He trusted Humphreys least of all because the man was black. Yet even that is an oversimplification. The tensions of their crime were beginning to take hold, and all suspicions assumed monstrous size. Comstock feared anyone who showed the slightest question of hs authority. He watched the men forward to be sure they acted as their normal selves. He was in recognizable danger every moment.

Payne wanted to get rid of Humphreys.

Oliver, who could lord it over Humphreys and no other, might have spoken up for the black man had he dared. But the Englishman was such a poor figure of a man that he did not have the guts to go against Payne and Comstock. Actually Oliver was already beginning to hate Comstock desperately, for Comstock had no use for the little man, and although Oliver was appointed second mate, whenever Comstock addressed him as "Mr. Oliver," Comstock's sarcasm was so obvious that none of the hands forward could miss the contempt.

All these factors were combined in the suspicions with which Comstock and the other two greeted Humphreys' story. All kinds of combinations could come to Comstock's mind: Payne and Oliver and Humphreys against him, or Oliver and Humphreys; or Humphreys promising the crew to kill Comstock and Payne.

All these possibilities revolved around one single fact. There *was* a gun. Humphreys *had* loaded it, and that Comstock knew for a fact because his own brother had told him so. No matter how they regarded each other, George was the one person whom Samuel Comstock could now trust to be honest with him.

Comstock weighed his crew. He considered the character of Gilbert Smith. In those grim moments between the time that Samuel had told George he would kill Smith and his reconsideration of Smith's unspoken plea that he be allowed to live, Smith had been discarded as a threat. Instinctively Samuel

Comstock knew that the real threat to his authority lay within his circle of mutineers. They were already tainted with the blood of the officers, and had nothing to lose in another murder.

Comstock made up his mind. That night in the cabin, he and Payne fixed it up between them. They consigned Humphreys to death. Oliver was not consulted; he was told. Then Comstock and Payne called Smith and Kidder in for one perfunctory conversation. Had they tried to seize the ship, or would they try? Smith and Kidder denied the charge whitely; they knew what would happen if they were not believed. But they were believed, for Comstock and Payne, each distrusting the other, also distrusted the black man Humphreys even more, and here was a chance to rid themselves of him.

Smith and Kidder were dismissed, and Comstock then chose a jury of four to try the case the next morning, with himself as prosecutor and magistrate. Payne, Oliver, George Comstock and Rowland Coffin were the jurors. Before the night ended, Payne went forward and told Comstock and Coffin privately that they were to find Humphreys guilty.

So the long night passed. The next morning the ship was moving southward at a fine clip in a northwest breeze that took them just where Samuel Comstock wanted to go. The sun shone brightly, and the heavens looked down, seeming to approve all that went on aboard the *Globe*. After the morning chores were done, the deck slushed down and the sails reset for the day's voyage, Comstock summoned the men aft to the quarter-deck. Oliver had armed a guard of six men who stood at attention with bayoneted muskets in their hands. Smith and Kidder were seated on a chest beneath the mizzenmast. Humphreys stood nearby, under the watchful eye of the heavily armed Oliver.

Humphreys must have known his fate already. When Comstock asked him what he had been doing down in the steerage with that pistol, the black man's answers were the same as before, but they were given in so low and indistinct a voice that the others had difficulty hearing what he said.

Comstock asked a few brief questions of Smith and Kidder. He scarcely seemed to listen to the answers, which were the same as they had made in the cabin the night before. But judging from the expression on their faces, these men were obviously not too worried about the outcome, although in the beginning Comstock had announced that someone was going to be hanged.

The case was presented in ten minutes. Comstock then summed up for prosecution, defense and the judicial system: "It seems that Humphreys has been found guilty in doing a traitorous and base act in loading a pistol, or was detected in the act of loading for the proposed act of shooting Payne and myself. But being detected, he has been tried and now the jury will give in their verdict. Guilty or not guilty? If guilty, he should be hanged to the studding rail boom shipped out eight feet on the foreyard. But if not guilty, Smith and Kidder should be put to the aforementioned gallows."

Comstock then looked at the jurors. They did not even bother to look at one another. Every juror spoke:

"Guilty."

"Guilty."

"I find him guilty."

"He is guilty."

With a glance of approval, Comstock discharged the jury to begin building the gallows. He turned his attention to the criminal. A cap was put on Humphreys' head and pulled down over his eyes. He was searched and the silver watch he had taken from the captain's chest was removed from his shirt. No need to send a perfectly good watch to Davy Jones. His pockets were turned out and the sixteen dollars he had stolen from the captain's sea chest were also confiscated.

Oliver, the captain of the guard, then led Humphreys to the bows, where he was forced to sit on the rail, his legs outboard. The noose was put around his neck.

But who was the executioner, who would do the deed?

There Captain Samuel Comstock had them. He told them that every man would do the deed—thereby sealing each into the bonds of the mutiny. For they were taking the law into their own hands, killing a man without the power of government, and for that all of them would at least have to stand judgment in a criminal court in America. Not a man failed to sense the immense importance of what mutineer Comstock was doing to them; he was welding his crew to the ship and himself as surely as if he had recruited them.

The executioner's rope was passed over the foreyard and trailed out on deck. Every man but Comstock put his hand to the rope, with orders that on the signal, which would be Comstock's striking of the ship's bell, they were to heave and hoist Humphreys out of this world.

Comstock stood straight, the bell ready.

"Have you anything to say, Humphreys? You have but fourteen seconds to live."

Humphreys swallowed hard beneath the executioner's cap. "When I was born I did not think I should ever come to this . . ."

Then Comstock struck the bell with his cutlass. The men heaved, and Humphreys' last words were cut off in a strangling gasp. The choking form of the steward twisted and turned. His manacled arms clutched upward for the rope until the head reached the foreyard. Then the kicking stopped. There was no groan, no further motion. One of the mutineers was dead. Less than thirty-six hours had passed since the mutiny began.

14

MUTINEER CAPTAIN

IMMEDIATELY AFTER the murder of Purser Humphreys, Mutineer Captain Samuel Comstock took steps to strengthen the chances of getting the ship to one of the Pacific islands.

On his cruise in the *Foster,* Captain Shubael Chase had sailed in and out of uncharted seas. Comstock knew that if he could find his island paradise, his hopes of living out his dream were good. Ridding himself of ship and crew, then he could settle in the life that beckoned him. But first he must use these instruments for his own salvation, and use them wisely or they might destroy him.

Having executed Humphreys, Captain Comstock put the purser's statements out of his mind. But the fact was that Humphreys had been truthful and honest, and when he was loading that pistol in the steerage he really did fear Smith and Kidder. The conspiracy against Comstock *did* exist, it was led by the pious Boatsteerer Gilbert Smith, who did not balk at lying to save his life or further his purposes. But Comstock, that strange combination of madness and religious training, would never believe that a true Christian like Smith could bring himself to tell a lie. Samuel and his brothers had lived too long under the shadow of the Friends to not know the proper paths of virtue.

Smith had pulled on the end of the execution rope, and so

had Kidder. In Comstock's mind, they had thus bound themselves to the mutiny. So Smith and Kidder could be forgotten; twice Smith had pledged his loyalty, and Kidder, as Payne and brother George both said, did not have the courage to act alone, no matter what was on his mind.

But there were others who might go astray. There was Columbus Worth, the captain's nephew. He must be adjudged a potential enemy to the mutiny, if only because of his heritage. There was Rowland Jones, the favorite of Captain Worth among the young boys, and his affection for the dead master must always make him a suspect in the future. There was Rowland Coffin, the cooper, a nephew of one of the owners; his stake in emotion and money was unknown but must be presumed to be high in favor of law and order.

It was by far best to assume that as captain he would now live in loneliness aft, as Thomas Worth had lived before, but that while Worth could presume that every man's hand was for the ship, Captain Comstock must presume that every man's hand was first for himself, and that no loyalty save that of fear would keep the others under his control.

Humphreys' body hung at the yardarm, swaying gently. "Cut him down!" Samuel Comstock shouted, and a man seized a boarding knife and slashed the rope through. But the hanging line tangled and fouled in the rigging as it fell, and had to be cut away again. Captain Comstock ordered a blubber hook fixed to the end of the line; it was done, and Humphreys' body began to sink as soon as it was cast away.

They were heading south and west. Stationing one man at the wheel, Captain Comstock gathered the men around the waist, where the helmsman and all others could hear, and he read out the new articles of the ship. He had prepared them the night before, spending long hours by lamplight in the cabin as he mulled over the Humphreys matter and the future.

In the bright sunlight, drawing his cutlass, Comstock traced an imaginary line down the center of the deck. "All right," he announced. "Those who are with us stay to the starboard side. Those who are not with us go over to the larboard."

Carefully, he did not say "those who are against us." The caution of the conspirator was setting in. The loyalists, the men who could not be expected to join the mutiny, outnumbered the mutineers by more than three to one. Comstock would not have batted an eye at killing each and every one of them and dumping them over the side, but he was careful not to arouse the frenzies of fear.

All grouped themselves against the starboard rail. Then Comstock read out his articles. Comstock was confirmed as captain. Payne was confirmed as first mate. Comstock and Payne would share two watches, and one-half the crew would be assigned to each watch.

These assignments indicated the state of affairs that existed aboard the mutiny ship, and how changed it was from the free and easy discipline of the whaler, for instinctively Comstock had gone to the war footing the naval vessel starboard and larboard watches, serving four hours on and four off, so that command could be exercised with a minimum of confusion.

Mutineer Comstock was committed to a life of unceasing vigilance, and to make the watchfulness possible, he now ordered that all members of the crew as well as the officers live and eat their meals in the cabin and the little staterooms occupied by the ghosts of the murdered officers. Some among the crew said their new captain was mad, but if he was, he had a cunning born of madness that served to protect him. In effect, he left himself open to betrayal for only four hours during each night—that was Payne's night watch—and thereafter during those hours Comstock would barricade himself in the captain's stateroom and sleep only fitfully.

Under Captain Worth, the men had done as they pleased about religion, but not under Captain Comstock. In the articles, Boatsteerer Smith was commissioned chaplain, regular services were scheduled, and the first of these was now to be held in commemoration of the lives of the murdered officers and the unfortunate Humphreys. The mutineers gathered aft, heads bowed, as they said prayers for the souls of the captain, the first mate, the second mate, the third mate and the black man. It was another move to make the men share Comstock's guilt, and Boatsteerer Smith, in his prayers for the murdered men, shared with the murderers the heaviest guilt of all. The mutineers, little by little, were being welded together with the men who had stood by innocently. The black stain of the mutiny was surging over them all, as the boatsteerer read from the Bible and the men sang hymns in praise of God and their departed brethren.

The Law of the Ship—articles—brooked no disobedience. Captain Comstock was the law, and there was no question about it. If any man saw a sail and did not report immediately, he was to be bound hand and foot and boiled in oil in a try-pot. If any man refused to fight a ship, he was to be boiled in oil in the same manner. So it was obvious what was on Captain Comstock's mind: detection and chase even before he could reach his objective.

As for the quarrels among the shipmates—for the mutiny made them all equals save Comstock and Payne, and, reluctantly, the sniveling Oliver—why, these must be settled in the future by trial at arms. Only thus, said the captain, could bad blood be wiped out and good will restored, as it had been from time immemorial by gentlemen everywhere. The risking of life at the end of a gun or sword washed out any and all injustice and created a man anew.

Each man of the crew was now ordered forward, to read or have read to him again the document that Samuel Comstock had prepared. Comstock signed himself with a flourish, lighted a stick of black sealing wax and dropped it down and fixed his ring into it. Then came Payne, and then Oliver, their seals black. Then came Liliston, Smith, and all the rest of them, including young George Comstock, and their seals were blue to differentiate them from the officers. If they had no rings, their thumb prints were affixed to the document. If they could not write their name, they scrawled an X.

After the ceremony Captain Comstock ordered the men to begin clearing the ship of whaling impedimentia. He announced that they were heading for the South Seas, where they could set up in independence and live a happy life. First thing to be done was to remove the stink of whale from the vessel of salvation.

So thousands of dollars' worth of spermaceti and whale oil were dumped over the side that day, the casks bobbing crazily in the sea. Some crew members began throwing over spades and whaling equipment, but Comstock reconsidered quickly and belayed that, because the metal weapons would be valuable for future trade with the natives they might meet.

Only Captain Comstock knew the course of the ship and where he was heading. He changed course a number of times, going east, west and south until he had everyone thoroughly confused except himself, and then he set them on the way to the general area he wished to explore to find his island. Their course was south and west, for in this direction, he recalled Captain Shubael Chase had passed through many an island group on that voyage of earlier years.

As if to remind the mutineers that they were not alone in the world, the god of storms turned loose his weapons on them the next morning. With the morning watch, Captain Comstock ordered all topsails down and reefs in the standing sails until the main was down to a third its normal size. It was a trying day, the wind lashing the rigging and the lee rail halfway under during the day watch. In midafternoon the strong north wind gusted and carried away the forward backstay to the main-topmast. That meant two men must go aloft in the threatening weather, and since they were all now equals, it was not easy to get the men to go up. But why should not

Oliver—or even Payne, for that matter—run up the mast and fix the stay if the wind was howling? It was not as if the mutineers had not been sleeping forward with the rest of them until a few nights earlier.

For two days and two nights they fought the Pacific storm in the cold and wet, and not a man aboard had more than an hour's sleep, so desperate were the winds and so strong the waves. But on January 31 the weather dawned fine, with scarcely a cloud in the sky, and the wind died down until they were sent along by only a pleasant breeze, north by east.

The storm had driven them almost due west. That noon Captain Comstock found their position to be 3°37' north by 170°6' west. So he changed course to southwest by west, and set the helm. No more dissembling. Comstock was eager to get where he was going, for now he felt they must certainly have left any possible pursuit generated by the *Lyra* behind, but that the second stage—search—might begin. There were few enough places in the world where a mutiny ship might head— the saga of the *Bounty* had shown that well enough. Those mutineers had sailed away to Pitcairn Island, not to be found for twenty years, but in 1808 Captain Mayhew Folger had discovered the place again, and since that time, with the large and increasing number of whalers abroad, hardly any lands at all remained unfound by the Western world. Because of this it was imperative that Comstock get to his destination, and get rid of the damning evidence of the ship.

For three days they steered southwest by west, and Samuel Comstock spent many an hour studying his charts and remembering the port, for they were approaching waters he had cruised with Captain Chase.

Then came an incident that took the captain's mind from the main problem. Liliston and Joe Thomas fell into a quarrel and threatened to take knives to each other. Here was the first opportunity for Captain Comstock to invoke his new code of conduct, and he did. The pair were sent to separate quarters, one to the forecastle and the other to the cabin, under guard.

Why all this folderol? asked Thomas, who was taken to the cabin and held.

Because that was the way it was, said the captain. They had known the price of quarreling after they signed the ship's papers. Now they were going to settle their quarrel like gentlemen and let there be no bad blood remaining.

He would shake hands with Liliston right there and settle the quarrel, said Thomas with feeling.

No, said the captain. The laws provided for a duel and there was going to be a duel.

Was it absolutely necessary? asked Thomas, whose hand had begun to quake.

Not only was it necessary, it was imperative, said Samuel Comstock, and set about loading his personal case of pistols. When Mate Payne entered the cabin, Comstock dispatched him to round up the crew and send them to the waist, where they would observe their first duel.

He loaded the pistols carefully with large charges of powder, but knowing his antagonists, he decided not to waste good bullets on such poltroons, so he tamped in wads of blank cartridges. But he said not a word to Thomas, who did not notice the preparations his captain was making. That perverse sense of humor of Comstock's was at work again, and he was about to play a monstrous joke on his fellow sailors.

Comstock led the quaking Thomas forward to the waist, while Payne brought Liliston up through the line of spectators. Chaplain Smith was called to say a prayer, and both men were enjoined to repent their sins and make their peace with God, since one of them was likely to be in his presence in the next ten minutes. Comstock presented each man with a pistol, set them back to back and counted off the paces for the duel. But Thomas was so frightened that as he whirled, his gun flew out of his hand and fell on the deck and exploded on impact. The wad struck Liliston in the ankle and he jumped in the air, shouting that he had been shot in the foot.

Liliston's second then clasped him, to succor the duelist. Comstock announced that as chief surgeon he would now operate to save Liliston's life. He went below for his surgical instruments, then laid them out on a blanket on deck. Before the smarting of the paper wad wore off Liliston was blindfolded (so he would not faint at the sight of his own blood) and the ankle was tied with a tourniquet, which soon cut off all feeling in his foot. Captain Comstock proceeded to strip the pants leg upward from the victim's foot. By this time, seeing that there was absolutely no blood, the bystanders were in on the joke, but Comstock put his fingers to his lips and set to work.

Liliston was moaning about the pain in his leg and calling on the memory of his mother.

"Hmmmmm," Comstock said, surveying the leg. "I guess I shall have to amputate to save your life, poor fellow"—and matching action to the word he began noisily sharpening a scalpel on his stone.

Liliston shuddered. He knew as well as the rest that amputation was almost always the price of a bullet wound in the extremities. He gathered his courage and waited for the worst.

"As wood is very scarce," Captain Comstock went on, deciding the charade was ended, "I do not see how we can afford you a wooden leg. You had better keep your present one until we reach some island where there is plenty of wood."

Thereupon Comstock had Liliston raised on his feet, and the tourniquet stripped off. As the man staggered on his numb ankle, Comstock gave him a swift kick in the rear with the side of his boot. "Now go forward and attend to your duty, and if I hear any more of your quarreling, I'll shoot you both," he said, and he assured the crew that the next time, however, the guns would be loaded, and that then he might also shoot the survivor of the duel.

So they sailed on, mutineer justice established, and apparently Captain Comstock had all his world under control.

Only George knew any different. George was aware of Samuel's habit of biting his fingernails when he was under great stress. These days, George noticed, Sam's fingernails were bitten down to the quick. One day Sam saw his gaze and laughed nervously. "I suppose you think I regret what I have done," he said to his brother. "But you are mistaken. I should like to do just such a job every morning before breakfast."

As he served in the cabin, George had another indication of the true state of affairs. Every night there was rum on the table, since the kegs below could be tapped with impunity. Comstock might control the lives of his mutineers, but he made no effort to control their drinking, that much was evident from the beginning. The habit that had brought Payne and Oliver to the Hawaiian Islands and left them high if not dry was one they were not willing to break.

The liquor did strange things to the conspirators. It loosened their tongues and sent them to bed with wild dreams. On the morning after Comstock had revealed to his brother that he had no conscience at all about the murders, Payne and Oliver complained of the dreadful nightmares each had suffered during the night. Captain Worth, Beetle, Lumbert and Fisher had appeared to one or both of them, horribly murdered as they had been, and the ghosts had frightened them both.

Mutineer Samuel Comstock laughed. "I know," he said. "Last night the captain appeared in my dream, too, and shook his gory locks and pointed at his bloody head."

The others were interested. "Yes," they said, "and then what?"

Comstock laughed uproariously. "I told him to go away," he said, "and if he ever appeared again I would kill him a second time."

15

LANDFALL

SOUTHWEST WAS THE COURSE and southwest they went, as fast as the wind and currents would let them travel, through high breeze and storm, luckily without encountering calm. February 6 brought another blow. The wind roiled up and the rain came down in sheets. Comstock ordered the three topsails double-reefed, and the helmsman to watch lively. Double watches were sent to the lookout stations, and the crew were kept moving all day and all night. Comstock was certain they were nearing land, and he did not wish to reach his tropical island in the dead of night and see his hopes shattered with the wreck of the *Globe* on a reef outside the lagoon.

The weather in the early-morning hours of February 7 was so dreadful that at two o'clock Comstock ordered the men to heave to so the ship could ride out the storm. The lookouts kept a sharp eye lest the *Globe* drift down on land. But no accident occurred. At six in the morning the storm abated and they made sail. Comstock set the helm west by south, and they moved ahead. He cautioned the lookouts: they should be coming to land soon. Sure enough, at eight-thirty that morning the forward lookout sang out that he had seen land, and the men all rushed to the forecastle to see what they could make out. Before them lay a green island on a blue sea, white beach shining in the sun.

They sailed steadily in toward shore, Captain Comstock considering if this might be the proper place. He sailed around and looked. The islands around them, he said, were a part of the Kingsmill group (now called the Gilbert Islands). They would not do at all, he could tell from a simple look over the shore: he wanted land for planting and lush vegetation, but all he could see was a handful of coconut palms. When the natives came out in their canoes to the slow-moving ship, he had the main taken aback and the *Globe* hove to. But even the natives were disappointing—small people, much darker than the Hawaiians, and with very crude canoes, compared to the double canoes and long graceful craft of the Polynesians. No, this was not the place. The natives held up beads and coconuts, but Comstock did not even stop to trade. They moved on outside for the night. In the morning the *Globe* was still off the island, Comstock observing. Only a twenty-foot beach, six-inch fish, canoes, coconut and breadfruit. He ordered the ship rigged to move on.

Heading northwest, they passed the channel between two other islands they called Marshall's and Gilbert's and hove to and sent a boat to Marshall's Island. But the boat did not get near land. The natives threatened them with fist and spear, and some swam out to try to snatch the boat's anchor and other bits of equipment. The swimmers grew so insistent that the men in the boat let fly with their muskets, and the dark heads disappeared beneath the water. The mutineers had no way of knowing how many, if any, they had killed or injured.

Two of the natives in a canoe had gotten between the ship and the boat. The men in the boat gave chase and when they hauled up on the canoe, the sailors fired into it, wounding one of the paddlers, perhaps mortally. He lay doubled up in the bottom of the canoe. The other held up a jacket of some kind and some beads imploring them not to kill him. The boatmen, chagrined at the exchange, rowed swiftly away, leaving the native in the bottom of the canoe and his companion, never looking back. Here was one more island that would not welcome a whaling captain again.

The boat came back to the *Globe*, was lifted aboard, and Comstock announced that they should sail off, leaving this island group. They headed for the islands they knew as the Mulgraves (which a later generation would call the Marshalls).

The next three days were near torture for the men of the *Globe*, because there was no way to tell how far they were from their destination. The weather blew a gale and the men before the mast were irritated about the delays. They wanted to make land. Comstock knew they must soon or he would have an ugly situation on hand. Then they came to an island chain he seemed to recall from that earlier voyage with Captain Chase. They stood off and tried to decide what they would do. At noon they came to an island that appeared to be what they wanted, and Comstock stood in but did not send a boat. A number of canoes appeared during the afternoon, and natives held up the usual fish and coconuts, breadfruit and bananas. They grinned and made friendly gestures. They were considerably lighter and larger people than those of the other group who had caused trouble, and Sam Comstock believed he could get along with these islanders. The men were extremely eager to get ashore, and Comstock knew they were going to be difficult if they did not. So he sent a boat ashore for trading, with Payne in it, and certain instructions. Payne soon came back with a boatload of women, while other women followed in a canoe. Here was a time-honored sailor's device for relieving the tensions aboard the whaler, and also for testing the behavior of the natives. If they would allow their women to consort with the sailors, then . . .

The native girls came aboard and disported themselves in waist, steerage and forecastle all night long; the rum flowed freely and many gifts and much loving were exchanged. When morning came, the girls good-naturedly popped over the side into the whaleboats and were put ashore with their presents of blankets, knives and iron hoops.

The men were tired of searching, and wanted to make their landfall here. But something told Sam Comstock no, this was not the place. The island was heavy with vegetation, but Comstock looked in vain for a place where he could plow and plant his seeds. So the ship was warped out to sea once again, many goodbyes were waved and the mutineers moved onward.

On the night of February 12 the *Globe* stood offshore, close-reefed and the watch tight lest she run aground in this island chain. The next morning the ship came to one atoll, low and narrow, where Comstock thought there should be a good anchorage. He was nearly exhausted from the long nights of vigil, unable to trust any man, and he wanted a rest which he could get only at anchor.

Comstock called to Payne to make ready the anchor, and the lead man stood in the chains to sound. The chain man called back that they had twelve fathoms, which was anchor depth, but on the next sounding he lost the depth altogether —no bottom. So Comstock moved in cautiously. They came to within a hundred feet of shore before they got a regular sounding, so deep was the water around this volcanic isle.

"Fourteen fathoms, no sand," said the lead man.

Comstock moved in.

"Ten fathoms and clear," said the lead man.

Farther.

"Seven fathoms and all clear."

"Anchor!" Comstock shouted.

"Heave her!" Payne shouted.

And the chains rattled as the heavy bower anchor went down forty feet to hit the rock and sit there.

Comstock ordered the sails furled, and the canvas was pulled down past the last reef and strapped firmly to the yards. A kedge was put astern to keep the *Globe* from drifting onto the beach. Then Comstock called for an anchor watch, which consisted of only two men, bow and stern, whose main task was to be sure they were not surprised by unfriendly natives. They were in the same group of islands where they had encountered the willing girls, so he expected no trouble, but he was not going to risk all he had done on a mistake now.

That night, for the first time in many a day, Captain Comstock climbed into his bunk. The men were happier now that they had found girls and the promise of more. The anchorage was deep and safe, and in a day or so he should be able to put things right.

The first mutineer slept very well.

16

LONG
LIVE THE KING

SAMUEL COMSTOCK was very near his goal, as he slept that night of February 13 in his purloined stateroom aboard the *Globe*. But elsewhere in the ship other men were sunk in gloom. On the morrow, Samuel Comstock had already announced there would be a search for their ultimate landing area. Then it was his intention to burn the ship and cut all ties to the past.

Young George Comstock lay in his bunk in the forecastle, where he had been allowed to return as Samuel began to feel more secure in the reins of power. George deplored the cruel turns of fate, and he wrote in his little diary:

"Oh how unfeeling must be the hearts of such wretches. They cannot be called anything better. . . .

"No name, no title is half revengeful enough. If the righteous are scarcely saved, where will these vile inhabitants of the earth go? Hell itself is not bad enough."

Strong words these, of a man for his brother, but George had seen the bloody head of Fisher and watched the throes of Mate Lumbert as he was dragged across the deck like a piece of meat and pushed over the side, then cruelly smashed in his last desperate grasp at life. Any brotherly feelings between George Comstock and the leading mutineer had long since vanished. All George hoped for from the old relationship was lenience, and perhaps a chance of escape. Then he remembered. It was Friday the thirteenth.

February 14, St. Valentine's Day, dawned. Here at the end of the world the mutineers spent the day searching for a suitable landing place, preferably near a cultivable area. The atoll off which they were anchored, Mili, was the island Samuel had chosen; he had the feeling he must stop and this place would do as well as any. In the morning a boat was sent east looking for the landing place, but came back to say all the shore was rocky. In the afternoon the boat went out to the west, and found the same conditions, so Samuel Comstock decided on this anchorage, rocky as it was. When the ship sank here, she could easily be put down in water deep enough to hide her forever.

February 15 was Sunday, but in spite of the honors Sam Comstock had paid Boatsteerer Smith in making him chaplain, Smith's talk of Sunday services was rudely disregarded. They must get to work, and there would be no more Sundays until the job was done. All hands were called and put to work to build a big raft out of spare spars and lumber. The whaleboats were too small and narrow for the task. Samuel Comstock wanted to take ashore everything of any value before he burned and sank the ship.

The raft was finished that day and anchored so that one end rested on the rocks at the shore; the other stuck out seaward, held in place by an anchor. This was the landing stage, and another raft was immediately built to carry goods to it. Two of the whaleboats were laid down, a little way apart, spars were put across them, then the spars were covered by boards which made an even flooring.

The men then began hauling up what they wanted from the holds and steerage. They took sails, to use for shelter, clothing and later perhaps for travel in the boats and canoes they would build. There was a brand-new mainsail and a foresail. They had a mizzen topsail and a spanker, a driver, a main-topgallant, two lower studding sails, a mizzen staysail, two mizzen topgallants and a flying jib, which someone said was torn and threw overboard in spite of his comrades' remonstrances. Comstock did not want anything thrown overboard. He could sense that these remnants of the civilization they had deserted might become treasures in good time. His theme was not the theme of the other mutineers. Comstock was thinking in terms of his islanders.

The unloading continued. Four casks of bread would last them several months, the men said. Eight barrels of flour, forty of beef and pork came off, then three casks of molasses, two barrels of sugar, one only part full; a barrel of dried apples, a cask of vinegar, two casks of rum, barrels of coffee, two chests of tea, a barrel of sour pickles, a barrel of cranberries and a box of chocolate.

Then came a cask of towline, three coils of cordage, a coil of rattling and one of lance warp, two balls of spun yarn and a ball of worming, plus a stream cable. Comstock knew that rope would be at a premium in the new life.

Off came the larboard bower anchor, all the spare spars that had not been used in the building of the rafts, and every chest of clothing, including those of the dead mates and the murdered Humphreys. Most of the ship's tools were taken this day; a few were left because something might have to be done before the ship was completely stripped and the hulk destroyed. That would come at the very end—but the end was nearly upon them, as any man could see.

As midday neared, and the number of shipments of supplies increased, Samuel Comstock went ashore to station himself there. He announced that he was doing this to maintain the security of the provisions, but as seamen came back to the ship to report to First Mate Payne and Second Mate Oliver, they said the captain was giving away their supplies to the natives.

Comstock *did* spend the day ashore. He *did* go off to the village with his natives. He *did* give them gifts, including bolts of cloth and trading goods and many items from the chests of the *Globe*. All day long he kept showing up at the landing station accompanied by various little knots of natives. He would pass out supplies and then accompany the natives back over the dunes and scrub to their village.

By nightfall every man of the *Globe* who had been involved in the movement of supplies had noticed the strange conduct of Captain Comstock. As they assembled under the eye of Cook Hanson to eat their chow on board ship, they had something to say. One of those who had been ferrying goods to shore all day said that he had seen Comstock tinkering with one of the whaleboats. When he asked the captain what he was doing, Comstock had been very vague, only saying he was thinking about making it larger.

All this information had an upsetting effect on Payne, who put down his kidd (bowl) and forgot to eat any more. The rest of the evening he was quiet and withdrawn.

Comstock did not come back to the ship. He had pitched a tent on shore. He said someone must stay there to guard the provisions and he would do it. That night he was very busy, but his object of attention was the native village not far away.

Already time was running out for the leader of the mutiny, just as surely as William Humphreys' fourteen seconds had run out. The fact of making a landfall had completely changed the positions of the mutineers. Before, Comstock's mastery of navigations had made it unthinkable that any other could challenge him. Now with the boat anchored at a friendly shore, he knew the men who had not taken part in the mutiny would be having second thoughts. He also knew that little Oliver was the devil's advocate, and that Payne feared Comstock as leader and would at some point challenge him, backed by the little Englishman. The only thing the others did not know was Comstock's plan to desert them and betray them to the natives, whom he would persuade to do away with them. That was his ace in the hole, but he had to move very rapidly if he was to succeed.

The next morning Comstock prepared to resume the unloading, but instead of a raft full of supplies, Payne sent a message. If Comstock and the unloading crew did not stop going to the native village and giving presents to the natives, Payne was going to quit and come ashore himself. He was particularly incensed because Comstock was giving away the fine shirts and clothing of the captain and the mates, items that would certainly be useful to them all in the months to come.

Here was the challenge, so soon.

17

THE KING IS DEAD

CHIEF MUTINEER COMSTOCK was hauling barrels of meat under the tent when the message arrived from Payne. He saw that the challenge of authority must be dealt with at once. Gilbert Smith and several others were helping; Comstock left the shore operations in the charge of Smith, the most trustworthy of them, and sent the whaleboat back to the ship for Payne. The order was that Payne come at once.

In a few minutes Payne arrived on the island accompanied by Oliver. They approached with a hangdog look about them. Comstock met them at the tent, and they moved inside, but the men outdoors could still hear.

"What do you mean by sending that message?" Comstock asked belligerently.

"Just what it said."

"Are you defying my authority?"

There was no answer.

Comstock spoke again. "I helped take the ship, and have navigated her to this place. I have also done all I could to get the sails and rigging on shore, and now you may do what you please with her; but if any man wants anything of *me*, I'll take a musket to him."

There it was, the reply to the challenge of his authority. Payne could either back down or stand up.

He stood up.

"That is what I want. I am ready."

Comstock's crisis was at hand. His own actions meant that any mutineer or sailor aboard could challenge any other. Payne was accepting his challenge, and so Comstock's authority over the ship was in balance.

He read his man. He knew the lantern-jawed, shambling Payne was slow of thought and hard as nails. Beside Payne stood his amanuensis and prompter, grinning evilly. Comstock's eyes narrowed, for he could see the truth in Oliver's glance—that they had been talking to the men, and they had support. If he killed Payne in a musket duel, he would still have all the rest of the men to deal with, and to deal with immediately and alone. There would never be another night's sleep for him surrounded by his comrades; there would not be a moment's rest when he could be off-guard.

It was too soon, but there was no recourse. He must put his ultimate plan into effect right now.

Comstock turned from the men and got into the whaleboat, ordering the rowers ashore to take him out to the ship. When he reached the deck he walked purposefully to the cabin, and then into his stateroom where the Laws were kept. He picked a cutlass out of the rack and chopped the paper to bits with it.

The men gathered around him in the cabin, and someone passed a remark to which Comstock took exception. The veins rose in his forehead and he shouted, "By God, I'll fight every one of you if I must. Get your weapons."

The men melted away before this fury and Comstock looked around for weapons. But before they left the ship, Payne and Oliver had concealed all the muskets and pistols, and the temper of the men was not such that Comstock dared ask any of them to lead him to the cache. It was time for action.

130

He picked up a cutlass scabbard and attached it to his belt, then sheathed the weapon. "This shall stand me as long as I live," he said to the men. "I am going to leave you; look out for yourselves."

The decision did not set badly with the other members of the crew, Payne and Oliver knew, but they were not sure enough of themselves to take the next obvious step—to murder the leader of the mutiny right there. Comstock went ashore again, taking what he wanted from the stores, and then disappeared into the palm jungle.

Payne took the boat and returned to the ship, greatly agitated, and broke out the muskets and pistols. He armed a number of the men with guns and extra ammunition, and led them ashore to picket around the tent and shoot at anything that moved out in the wilderness.

Comstock's negotiations with the natives did not bear the immediate fruit he had hoped, one reason undoubtedly being the whites' possession of all those firesticks, so the next morning Comstock felt he had to try to reassert authority or to somehow negotiate. Meanwhile, Payne was waiting at the tent and talking about what was to be done. He asked Boatsteerer Smith to pick up a gun and be the one who would shoot Comstock dead the next time they saw him. Smith stood on his chaplain's rights and demurred.

Dawn broke over the island with its misty glow, and then the wisps began to rise off the water, and the sun came into view over the headland beyond, and day was there. Shortly after sunrise the ship's crew was up, and the men ashore were being replaced as guards. Off in the distance on the hill, Payne saw Comstock coming down to them, alone, his cutlass in his hand.

"Who will shoot him?" Payne shouted and little Oliver stood forth. He loaded up several muskets. When he had done so, three others of the crew volunteered to help murder their man, and they leveled their guns as Comstock came up.

The ground sloped down and then up again. He seemed wrapped in thought, his eyes on the ground. Suddenly, just as he came within musket range, he noticed the guns pointed at him.

He waved the cutlass and his bare hand at his old companions. "Don't shoot. Don't shoot me! I will not hurt you."

But little Oliver, his face twisted in a grimace of pure hate, shouted "Now!"

Four muskets rang out.

Comstock fell and rolled down the hill, the cutlass dropping from nerveless fingers. They went toward him, Payne first, with an ax in his hand, and so fearsome was the body of the mutiny's leader that Payne first buried the ax in Comstock's skull before the others dared approach and touch him.

There were two bullet wounds from the four shots, either of which would have been instantly fatal. One had hit him in the upper lip and gone through his head. The other had hit him in the right breast, then passed diagonally out near the backbone. Payne and Oliver approached as carefully and stiffly as fighting dogs over a fallen enemy, and poked and prodded until they were sure Samuel Comstock was stone dead. Then with great relief they called all hands to shore.

Rejoicing in their deliverance, the mutineers and their accomplices sewed the body up in a canvas sack. The others were put to work in shifts digging a grave. Payne looked around for a place: there was one site that Comstock had spoken of as the place he would put the church in this new town he had talked so wildly of establishing here on the shore of the Pacific. The church site, that's where they would bury their fallen leader.

Comstock's body was laid in the grave, dressed in all his clothes and wrapped in the American flag, with the cutlass beside him. All they took from him was a watch he would not need where he was going.

An honor guard fired muskets over the grave, and Gilbert

Smith, adopting his role of chaplain, read the fourteenth chapter of Isaiah. It was almost touching, and sad. Then, at a signal from Payne and Oliver, who stood with muskets charged and watched them, every member of the crew was forced to dance on Samuel Comstock's grave.

Only young George Comstock refused, and out of a feeling for fraternal piety, the mutineers let him live in spite of it.

18

THE NEW ORDER

TWENTY-TWO DAYS had passed since the fatal moment when Samuel Comstock led the three mutineers into the captain's cabin of the *Globe,* and now the men's lives changed for the third time. They were under the command of the two beachcombers, Payne and Oliver, and they had no confidence in the character or leadership of either one. Comstock was evil but he was a leader, and he had presented his men with a plan to establish some sort of life for themselves.

The new leaders had no plan. Before becoming mutineers, they had been common seamen. Before that they had practiced the arts of the beachcomber, and neither had ever distinguished himself anywhere except by bravado and anti-social behavior. Neither had a smidgen of navigation or geographic knowledge; they had no science or profession; they knew nothing of agriculture; they had no other skills.

The men of the *Globe* sensed this and fell into despair. Boatsteerer Smith prayed long and hard for all their souls and for the rescue of their bodies. They were willing, all but the two mutineers, to be found immediately and taken back to Nantucket, blessed Nantucket, and they were willing to stand before their peers to explain their conduct.

Boatsteerer Smith did more than pray, however. The coun-

terplot that he and Peter Kidder had begun hatching the day
after the mutiny was still in their minds. All Smith and his associates wanted was a chance. Those associates included George
Comstock, who had long since lost all love for his brother
Samuel, Stephen and Peter Kidder, plus the two boys, William
Lay and Cyrus Hussey. Smith had not been confident enough
of Rowland Jones and Rowland Coffin and others to approach them; only secrecy had so far saved the little band
from the same fate that Humphreys had met. Only secrecy
and action would save them now. What Smith wanted was a
chance to break away with the ship before the mutineers could
get around to burning her. Just a chance, that was all the
counterplotters expected.

The affair of the morning of February 17 had disinclined
anyone of the crew from further work, and so Payne declared
a holiday, hoping to cement his authority and also to give
himself some time to think about the future.

After a suitable interval, a handful of natives appeared at
the tent, bringing bananas and coconuts and breadfruit, indi-
cating they wanted to trade, not fight. They were brown-
skinned, middle-sized, with broad faces and flat noses, dark eyes
and large mouths, and jet-black hair which they wore long and
coiled up in a bun. Most of the older men wore beards. Men and
women wore little else; the men put a wide belt around their
waist, from which suspended a pigtail fore and aft. The
women also wore belts, with bits of tapa cloth about the size of
a pocket handkerchief before and behind. Above the waist both
sexes went naked, except in cold, when they put on a sort of
shawl.

This morning represented the first contact of the mutineers
with the natives, for on the previous days Samuel Comstock
had done all the talking with the people of the island.

They came then, and they entered the tent, to feel the canvas and examine the poles. They touched everything inside,
and they marveled and they giggled and they sat down to talk

sign language with the sailors. Someone opened the rum, and soon the campsite was one huge party, each sailor with a willing girl beneath his arm, and a mug of rum in his hand. Payne and Oliver stood a little apart for a time, oppressed by the responsibility they had assumed, but not for long. Having assigned watches, and warned against drunkenness, they fell to with a will. Payne found himself a girl, who signified that she came from some other island. She suited him beautifully, and under the influence of a few tots of rum he seemed to suit her as well.

So the festivity continued into the night. They had ship's biscuit and beef and pork and all the other edibles that had been brought ashore. The natives dug a pit and cooked breadfruit, bananas and fish on hot stones, and the night was filled with laughter and merriment.

As darkness fell, Payne sent Boatsteerer Smith and five others who seemed to hang back from the festivities to the ship, to get them out of the way, and to take charge of unloading further the next day. Besides Smith they included George Comstock, Stephen Kidder, Peter Kidder, Joseph Thomas and Anthony Hanson. Smith would much have preferred to have his other two conspirators with him, young Lay and Hussey, but for them to ask to go aboard would have been to court suspicion, so it was left that the two boys would find the first opportunity to swim out to the ship, and then they would board as the ship got under way. Thomas and Hanson were suspected, in various degrees, of being sympathetic to the mutineers, Thomas in particular because of his quarrel with Captain Worth that set off the murders. So they were told nothing while Smith made his preparations, but were encouraged to bunk out while the others stayed on watch.

Smith went below to the steerage and found there one musket that had been overlooked by Payne, three bayonets and some whale lances. He brought these up on deck and laid them handy in case they would be needed to fend off their ship-mates. He put the two Kidders and George Comstock to work clearing the running rigging, getting the sails free so a jerk of a line would put them into action.

Smith then greased a saw and took it up to the windlass, where it would be handy to cut through the cable. One hatch-et remained aboard, and he put this down by the mizzenmast, where it could be used to cut the stern moorings, after the bow was freed and the ship swung off-shore.

Taking one man, Smith climbed up into the fore-topsail yard, loosed the sail from its fastenings and turned out the reefs while two of the others loosened the main-topsail in the mainsail. All this was done silently, in the darkness before the rising of the moon, and the conspirators prayed that their movements would not be noticed, for seeing the sails come up, the mutineers and their party must know precisely what was happening.

Then Smith saw it—the moon beginning to peep up, and he hurried. They were waiting for the two boys, Hussey and Lay, but they could wait no longer. Smith sent a man into the fore-yard and another onto the fore-topsail yard. Their task would be to loosen the bunts of the sail from their gaskets on the signal *let fall.*

Down below, Smith looked at his watch in the light of the binnacle flame, and saw that it was nearly half past nine, the time for moonrise. The sky looked it too, and so with a farewell glance ashore at the two sturdy souls he must leave behind him, Boatsteerer Smith moved forward to the windlass and picked up the handsaw. Quietly, forcefully, he worked, and in two minutes the cable was cut, and the ship was moving against her stern line. She payed off in a hurry, and in a minute or so her head was off the land.

Aft the hawser was cut, freeing the stern moorings. The ship swung into the wind, the sails went up with a pop, and

Smith cut loose a raft of iron hoops which were beginning to tow alongside.

The six men of the *Globe* set out to sea, to find their way home again and perhaps to save the other nonmutineers from a long, wasted life or an inglorious death. They were undertaking a dangerous voyage, Smith and his mates, for all he and the others knew of ship management was what they had observed. As to the niceties of navigation and course plotting, not a man aboard knew anything. Smith knew only that by steering east he would somewhere run into the Pacific coast of the Americas, and that became his goal. The question was: Would the provisions hold out, and could the men?

19

THE
NATIVES OF MILI

WILLIAM LAY AND CYRUS HUSSEY could hardly contain themselves on the evening of February 17, so eager were they to
slip away from the party in the tent and join their friends
aboard the *Globe*. They knew the attempt would be made that
night, it had to be, for it was the night of carousal that made it
possible for Smith to move a hundred-foot craft out past the
noses of nearly a dozen men without their knowing it.

When the moon came up, one quick look told Lay and
Hussey all they needed to know. There in the distance, limned
against the night, they saw their ship, main fore and mizzen
sails and the topsails and even the flying jib beginning to flare
out. They said nothing. It was best to let someone else discover
the train of events, for then they would not be suspect. Sure
enough, not half an hour after the *Globe* sailed, up came the
cry: "The ship has gone!"

The alarm was raised by the two men set to guarding the
campsite against the natives. They had either dozed off or
were otherwise occupied, perhaps with charm, but as the moon
came up full, it shone directly on the place where the *Globe*
should have been—and was not. In a moment every man was on
the beach, staring seaward. For even though Payne and Oliver
had intended to burn the ship, there was something about her

sturdy frame that was a link with home. If she was gone, then where were they? Castaways on a desert isle.

Payne and Oliver put the best face on the matter that they could: they suggested that night that the ship had somehow drifted away from its moorings, that Smith and the ungrateful wretches of the crew had broken into new-found rum or had gone to sleep on watch, and that next morning on the change of tide, the ship would miraculously reappear. But even Oliver did not believe it as Payne said it; in their hearts they harked back to the charge of poor William Humphreys and they knew the black man's words had been the truth, that they had sent him to his death for nothing.

At dawn every man was up, straining his eyes across the sea, but there was nothing to be seen save a handful of gulls riding outside the surf, and the green and white and yellow fronds of the palm trees waving along the shore. The *Globe* was gone.

Payne tore off his cap and flung it on the ground before him. He swore a mighty oath and promised that if that holy-stoning, sanctimonious, fraudulent parson Gilbert Smith should ever come into his presence again, he would hang him high from the foretop yardarm if it took a week to do it. The same went for the other five men aboard the *Globe*. Payne and the others had trusted these men and they had been betrayed.

This morning, almost immediately the mutineers' camp was surrounded by scores of natives. They had been summoned from all the islands of the Marshalls to take a look at the white men who had come in their great ship, and a number of chiefs had come to Mili to see the whites themselves and to consult. These Marshall islanders were quite surprised when Payne informed them that the great ship had left and would not return. The announcement diminished the awe the island-ers had for the whites considerably and when they asked what had happened to Comstock, the first man they had seen, they got no more satisfactory answers out of Payne either.

Payne and the others did not know it, but already their situation was becoming hazardous as the Marshall islanders learned they were not creatures of great power, but men like themselves, although very different in small ways. However, Payne was quick to show the natives his muskets, and they knew what those instruments were and regarded them with respect.

Comstock had opened his bags of tricks, so to speak, and let the natives choose what gifts they would have. Those who had come to him had returned to their villages and spoken of the white man's generosity. Now the hand of Comstock was still heavy upon the shoulders of the mutineers, for the natives came in and began to help themselves out of the ship's stores in boxes and barrels piled inside the tent and under canvas alongside.

For a time Payne was musing over events and he paid the natives little attention. His first concern was the loss of the ship and what that meant. He and Oliver had everything to lose if the ship had not drifted away. He firmly suspected that Smith and his companions intended to sail the ship to some port. If and when they succeeded, then it would be only a matter of time before naval vessels would be on the prowl. Eventually the mutineers would be found, if they stayed in so populated a place as Mili.

Thus Payne turned immediate attention to the whaleboats which were ashore. He had two of them, and he now proposed that Coopers Coffin and Hussey supervise the conversion of two boats into one, bigger and with raised sides, so they could sail among the islands and find a safer place in which to hole up.

Coffin turned to with a will that excited some suspicion in the minds of William Lay and Cyrus Hussey. Perhaps Coffin was only making the best of a bad situation, but Lay had the definite impression that Coffin knew more about the mutiny from the very beginning than he had let on, and that his sympathies were with the mutineers. Cooper Hussey did not seem to share these thoughts, but his mind was a thousand miles away. He was considering now just how much chance the others had of getting to a civilized port, and how long it would be before they could expect to be rescued.

On the night that the ship disappeared, Payne had made his first serious social error, which was the beginning of a change in all their lives. He knew that the girl he had chosen as his bedmate was from another island, but he did not know that she was married to one of the Mili natives. The Mili marital code was not strict, and cooperation with a white foreigner was never envisioned in it one way or the other, so what happened under the influence of rum was one thing; but the next day when the girl decided to go home to her husband and Payne stopped her, it became something else. He not only restrained her, he beat her when he caught her sneaking out of the tent, and when she did so a third time he put leg irons on her and chained her to the tent pole.

The Mili islanders considered it scandalous that the white men would behave in such a fashion, but the white men still had a godlike quality to them because of the great ship, and this carried Payne and the others on. The word about the strangers had spread to every corner of the atoll, and men, women and children kept appearing at the tent to see them. The natives were still friendly to the American sailors, trading food for iron hoops and nails and whatever else the mutineers and the companions could spare.

The work continued on the whaleboat, and made some progress. On February 19 Lay and Hussey and several of the other young fellows got permission from Payne and Oliver to make a trek around their atoll. It would be useful, they told the authorities, and Payne agreed that it might. So the young men crossed over the coral reefs from one low-lying islet to another, it being low tide, and followed tracks in the sand until they came to a medium-sized village about seven miles

away on another atoll. What a circus they made for the islanders! The villagers gave them cooked breadfruit and coconut
milk, but they stood around them in a circle, the children's
eyes bugging out, and they stared and stared. Hussey, in particular, was an object of interest because of his hair, bleached
golden by the tropic sun. Blond hair and white skin made him
a sensation.

Payne was eager to get the work on the boat finished, for he
wanted to put the Marshalls behind him; he would feel far
safer at a landfall of his own choosing. Still, the mutineers were
only two and the nonmutineers were more than three times
as many, so when the young fellows asked for favors they were
usually granted. Oliver spent much of his time near the rum
cask, until finally on Payne's orders Hussey stove in the head
of it. The two, Payne and Oliver, also spent much of their
time seeking young women, and the manacled girl was finally
let go.

On February 20 Payne ordered Coffin, Hussey and the rest
to get to work on the boat transformation, but they said they
wanted to explore the atoll some more, and Payne was so
bemused that he let them go. Two or three of the men went
to the village, taking muskets with them which they fired to
astound the natives. In the long run this was very bad policy,
producing fear, although in the short run it seemed good
policy, producing awe.

Payne and Oliver took three men and set out in one of the
boats to explore the island, leaving the others behind to wait
and guard the supplies. That night William Lay went into the
village where they had been treated so well, and found that he
was still welcome there. One man, about sixty years old,
pressed him to go to his house and spend the night, which Lay
did. After the evening meal there, he lay down on sleeping
mats with the rest of the family. Then rats came in, sweeping
through the place like a plague. They ran over his feet and
they nibbled his shoes. They came so close to his face that he

was scared, and they gave him altogether a thoroughly miserable night. He found from his new friends that rats were the only four-legged animals on the islands. The natives were used to them; they did not eat them except in dire need, but they subsisted mostly on fish, bird's eggs, bananas, coconuts and the inevitable plantains and breadfruit.

Lay enjoyed his visit with this Marshalls family. He gave them some gifts from his pockets, and they seemed to appreciate them. Then, at ten o'clock in the morning, he went back to the tent, hoping Payne and Oliver were still away or they might become angry with the lack of discipline at the campsite. But Payne and Oliver were not the disciplinarians that Comstock had been, either of the men or of themselves.

Shortly after William Lay returned, surrounded by natives, Payne and Oliver came back in the boat, bringing with them two young women whom they now called their wives, to warn off the other sailors. They settled down to a life of roistering, and that very day the idea of the watch was forgotten. Why would they need a watch, Payne said, when the natives were so friendly?

The next morning Payne was not so pleased. He discovered that his "bride" had decided to go back to her village. He searched high and low but found no sign of her. He and Oliver took muskets and pistols and cutlasses and rushed into the village to demand the return of Payne's "wife." Since it was still dark, they secreted themselves outside a big hut and waited until the natives awakened. Then they burst into the place and found the girl. They fired blank cartridges into the hut and frightened the natives so that they fled. Payne and Oliver took chase, caught the girl Payne wanted and dragged her back to the camp. When she protested and pleaded and began to struggle, Payne beat her up and then put her in irons. From that day on he kept her in irons so she would not escape again.

The villagers were angered when they learned of the plight

of the girl. They acted quickly enough, too, for the next morning when Payne looked at the tool chest of the ship, he saw that the lock had been forced and a hatchet and two chisels were missing. This *was* a serious matter, since they were busy remodeling one of the whaleboats. Before, the natives had taken what they wanted, but this was a different matter, and if the thief did not return all the articles, Payne said, he was going after him and seek vengeance.

All day long Payne harangued the visiting natives with his story. They understood him well enough when he acted out the drama of the smashed tool-chest lock. They apologized in their own way for the bad behavior. But at the end of the day, the tools still were not returned. As Payne and Oliver talked about what to do, a native came in with one half of one chisel. The fact that the tool had been broken infuriated Payne once again, and he put the helpful villager in irons. The next day, Payne said, that man would go with the white men to the village, find the thieves and the tools, and Payne would punish the offenders. That night, other natives filed in and out of the tent with the shackled prisoner, but they indicated no displeasure, nor any emotion at all.

In the morning Payne sent Rowland Coffin, Rowland Jones, Cyrus Hussey and Thomas Liliston to recover the tools. They were to escort the prisoner to the village, make him lead them to the hut of the thieves and return with hatchet, chisel and thief. Payne had such little fear of the islanders that he refused to give the men bullets for their guns. They each carried a musket, powder and some bird shot. That was all.

The posse went up the hill from the camp and over toward the village, escorting the manacled prisoner. When they reached the village he pointed to one hut, and they entered, searched and found the hatchet. Their prisoner would not name the thief and they did not know what else to do, so they prepared to return with the hatchet and let Payne decide the next step.

What a fool Payne had turned out to be! For in his harsh treatment of the native girls he had shown the people of the Marshalls that he was not to be respected if he was to be feared. And in his threats against the villagers he had aroused their instinct for self-preservation.

The four musketeers left the Mili village with the hatchet, but they had not reached the halfway point to their camp when they saw a hundred natives running after them. If they had been given bullets and could have fired, to kill or wound one man, they might have made a stand. Even had they stood and fired their bird shot at the advancing band, they could have stung some of the natives enough to stop them. That was what Payne had in mind—a show of force without any deaths. But if Payne had been a good leader he would have been there in the men's hour of need. As it was, they were alone, and they panicked and ran.

The Mili natives were adept at throwing stones, and now a rain of rocks, each the size of a man's fist, poured upon the men of the *Globe*. Hussey, Coffin and Liliston rushed on, but Jones was struck on the back by a rock and fell down. The last Hussey saw of him, a native was bending over Jones's recumbent form, lifting a rock to bash out his brains.

The three survivors tore down the hill and entered the tent to deliver their breathless report. Payne and Oliver handed out muskets and cutlasses, and the men of the *Globe* prepared for a siege behind the boxes of provisions.

The natives, coming down the hill slowly, did not attack, for they had seen the weapons of the Americans. Instead the group that had killed Jones settled down not far from the seamen to hold a council. More and more natives kept coming in, so it was obvious that the word of trouble had reached every corner of the atoll.

For an hour there seemed to be a stalemate, but then the islanders came up with a master stroke: they advanced and began to tear one of the boats to pieces. Payne grew very agitated;

here was his lifeline being destroyed before his eyes. He put down his gun and cutlass with great ostentation and advanced toward the islanders, in a quiet, almost friendly way. One man met him and they sat on the ground for a few moments and talked in sign language and broken English. Then Payne disappeared into the midst of the natives.

He was gone for an hour. When he returned to the *Globe* camp he announced that he had saved their lives, but just barely. The islanders wanted everything they had, without exception. They also demanded that Payne and his friends adopt the island way of life and subject themselves to the island laws.

The natives surrounded the tent with war clubs and javelins in hand. They began moving in, taking what they wanted, breaking into boxes and tins and barrels. One began to pull down the tent itself. With this the islanders became very agitated, and whooped and brandished spears and clubs. Payne believed he had saved himself. He went willingly outside the tent with two natives. With a rush, then, the others were on the place. William Lay was grasped firmly by the arms. On one side he recognized the man who had befriended him at the village two nights earlier; on the other side was the man's wife. They dragged him away and he thought they were about to kill him, but they took him into the bushes and held him fast, watching the violence as it unfolded.

The first man killed was Columbus Worth. An old woman ran him through with a spear and then smashed his head with stones. That was the pattern thereafter. Liliston ran, and was stoned down and then beaten to death. Oliver made it to the bushes some twenty-five yards from the tent, before he was hit from behind by an accurate stone thrower, and then killed. Joe Brown, the Sandwich islander, rushed for the water in which he was as much at home as a human being could be, but he was overtaken in the water by a spear and killed.

Payne thought he was safe, but his captors took up stones.

149

One struck him in the head. He ran. Then he was brought down by a stone in the back and killed like the rest.

All this was accompanied by the most piercing yells and screams that Lay had ever heard. He became terrified and expected death at any moment. But his protectors flung themselves down on him, held him securely and would not let him look at any more of the carnage.

One islander came by their clump of brush and made a pass at Lay with a handspike he had picked up in the wreckage of the tent. The old man and the woman protected him again; they shouted at the other and he slunk away. Then they came out of the brush, took Lay by the hand, and pushed and pulled him along to the village. His feet were bare and they were badly cut on the coral rock. He wanted to stop and soothe his bleeding feet, but the old couple urged him on and kept looking back as if fearing pursuit. Finally they reached the village and the old man's hut. They went inside and were met by a noisy, shouting mob. Lay still expected that the end would come at any moment, and he sat half paralyzed by the prospect. Then, through the door, he saw more islanders approaching the hut, and in the middle of them, his blond-haired friend Cyrus Hussey. He knew instinctively that they were the only two survivors of the massacre. The *Globe* had claimed its own this day.

20

THE LONG
VOYAGE HOME

As soon as the *Globe* had moved out of reach of Silas Payne and John Oliver, the six seamen who manned her heaved a collective sigh of relief in the gathering moonlight, and headed for deep water and the east.

They still had a compass aboard, through Smith's artful machinations. Earlier, when he delegated them to stay aboard the vessel, Payne had had an inkling that some attempt might be made to escape, so he insisted that the two compasses be removed from the ship and brought ashore. There were, in fact, three compasses, unbeknownst to the untrained mutineer: the binnacle compass, one other standard compass, and a floating compass above the captain's bunk which he used to tell him whether or not the ship was on course. By substituting that last compass for the binnacle, Smith had fooled Payne into believing he had all the navigation instruments on shore, and that deception lulled the mutineer.

After warping out and setting the helm for the east, Gilbert Smith paused for a bit to take stock of his situation. It was not good, and yet it was not desperate. There was still food on board, not a great variety, but a supply of biscuits and good meat, and some other staples that would get them through if they did not take too long. Valparaiso was the whaler's main port of call on the Pacific coast of South America. Smith would head for this port.

From the beginning of this adventure, the four who had shipped from Nantucket comprised one party on the vessel, and the two beachcombers, Thomas and Hanson, made another. Hanson, the cook, was amenable enough, although Smith, the two Kidders and George Comstock never really accepted him as one of them. He was a Barnstable man, at least, and that gave him a half-hearted welcome to the group of offshore islanders.

Joseph Thomas was the troublemaker. He was surly and independent. Almost immediately he began quarreling with Gilbert Smith and questioning his authority. The others soon put him to rights on *that*—after all they had gone through, they recognized that no ship can have more than one captain, and Smith was the man best suited for the task. But Thomas made trouble for Smith, just as he had made trouble before for Captain Worth and all the others he dealt with. He shirked his work. He complained about the food. He tried to stir up others to complain about Smith's authority.

In the evenings, when the ship's canvas was drawing well and there was nothing to do but gaze eastward and hope, the men talked about the mutiny. They were careful, even among themselves, because they recognized the legal dangers they all faced.

Gilbert Smith was certainly innocent. All could remember what he did on the night of the murders, and if his actions were not brave or brilliant, at least they were not treasonable. George Comstock could recall how Smith came up to the hatchway and looked down to see the mutineers in action, then turned and hid until Comstock went away. The others could remember how Smith had arrived in the forecastle, all disheveled and in his underclothing, to ask their advice on where he should hide from Comstock, who was coming to kill him.

The Kidder brothers' actions were totally unexceptionable

during the mutiny. They had spent the whole night in the fore-castle. They were the fomenters of the movement to take the ship back, and had enlisted Smith as the most knowledge-able of the crew to help them.

George Comstock had already proved how sickened he was by the mutiny. All knew that he had been at the helm and that his brother had threatened him with death if he changed course or aroused the officers. He had been forced that night to put the noose around Mate Lumbert's feet and drag him up the companionway stairs, punishment enough for being Comstock's brother.

Hanson had been asleep in the cook's quarters in steerage and as soon as he could get his trousers on he had joined the others at the forecastle; there was no question about his activities.

But there was question about Joe Thomas'. Just how much did Thomas know about the mutiny? Smith was of the opinion that Thomas knew a good deal about it, and that if he had been an honest sailor he would have reported immediately to the officers. Yet it was complicated. George Comstock said that a remark dropped by his brother had indicated Samuel was planning the mutiny a month before it happened. Had Thomas known all that time? The beachcombers shipped on the *Globe* on December 8. From certain remarks that Thomas made, the others began to believe the plot was hatched even before the recruits joined the ship.

The suspicion that Thomas had known all about the mutiny grew as the voyage continued, and the men edged away from him. They also turned over in their minds the conduct of the others aboard the ship. Rowland Coffin came in for consider-able suspicion, because he had seemed very familiar with the mutineers and sympathetic to them all the way along. The "jury" that had been appointed by Comstock to try William Humphreys had consisted of Payne, Oliver, George Comstock and Coffin. Payne and Oliver were obvious choices; George could be excused because he was a mere boy, deathly afraid of his brother. But why Coffin? Peter Kidder said Coffin knew about the mutiny and had told him so. Gilbert Smith agreed. He also was certain that after the mutiny Coffin had spied on the rest of them and told the mutineers everything that happened.

They all put down Thomas Liliston as a mutineer, for several of them had seen him coming back to the forecastle carrying a hatchet and knife as Comstock went to the cabin. The fact that Liliston had lost his nerve at the last moment would not save him.

As the men of the *Globe* sailed on, musing worriedly about the future and their own fates, the month of March passed, and April, and May, and still they saw no land but an island or two. On the leg of the Pacific where they were traveling there were few enough of those islands, not even rocks that would give sanctuary to a handful of birds. But as long as the food and water held out, they would last.

Those three and a half months brought desolation to the ship. She had started out with little enough; now her canvas was tattered and torn and they could not mount all the sails. They had even become so dispirited that they abandoned the early practice of keeping one watchman aloft to look for sails or a landfall. They did their work, they set the sails, they trimmed them in heavy weather. They headed east, and they waited.

At long last, one June morning their vigil was rewarded. A man working in the bow looked up, and there ahead of them he saw the purple haze and elevated horizon that meant land. They embraced, they danced on the deck, and they smiled for the first time in weeks. Land meant rescue and rescue meant home.

Gilbert Smith still had his problems. He had to find a port and bring the ship in. With his little crew, working the ship in close waters would be very difficult. And even before that, what was he to do? They did not want now to wreck the *Globe* on a reef, having brought her so far.

Gilbert Smith had applied himself to the books in the captain's cabin and had gained some rudimentary knowledge of navigation. In fact, his dead reckoning had been remarkably accurate, because although he did not know it, he had navigated the ship for seventy-five hundred miles to within thirty miles of Valparaiso. Having to make a decision, Smith turned north and sailed along the coast, hoping to sight a ship that would give him his position and send some men aboard to work the *Globe* into shore.

On the morning of June 5 the men of the *Globe* saw a sail. They signaled. They steered for the other ship. They hailed and got a response from the vessel, which was a Chilean coaster. The captain had a few words of English, so Smith was able to make known his troubles and his needs. But the Chilean's problems were almost as serious as the *Globe*'s: the men were half starved and had no food to spare. The Chileans turned over a sheep and some potatoes, while Smith in exchange gave them twenty-one bags of bread and four chunks of salt beef. But the Chilean captain did send some men aboard, and while half of them did not understand a square rigger and were therefore useless, the others were of enough help, and with the advice of the Chilean captain, Smith was able to bring the *Globe* safely into Valparaiso harbor. Inside the port, when told the story of the mutiny, harbor officials immediately were suspicious. Their faces grew grave. All of the survivors, from Smith to Thomas, were clapped in irons and taken aboard a British man-of-war that lay in the harbor.

The port authorities then got in touch with Michael Hogan, the American consul in Valparaiso. There was some talk of hanging these mutineers at the yardarm, so strong was the feeling of officialdom against murder at sea. But in the person of Consul Hogan, the men of the *Globe* had a fortunate circumstance. He was not the usual type of State Department official at all. His job was commercial, and in it he served the interests of the shipowners and traders, but he was not blind to the faults of American business abroad.

"My experience for upwards of three years in this port," he wrote Secretary of State John Quincy Adams, "has proved to my conviction that the masters of merchant ship trading here are oftener in error than the sailors, who, by severe inconsiderate and unfeeling treatment, are driven to insubordination and desertion. . . ."

Hogan was a good man for the investigation of the *Globe* mutiny, for he did not begin automatically with the assumption that Captain Worth was all right and the men were all wrong. He set out to get the facts.

He started with the least obvious. On June 9 Consul Hogan had Stephen Kidder brought from his prison ship to the consulate and asked searching questions about the mutiny. Had there been any signs of mutiny before the second sailing from the Hawaiian Islands? Who besides the mutineers knew of the mutiny? Then Hogan settled down to the dangerous questions. Had Kidder heard the noise of the murders? And what happened to the captain and First Mate Beetle?

If Kidder had been able to describe their fates in detail, it would have gone bad for him because the bodies of the captain and mate were never seen by most of the crew. Kidder answered the questions honestly and thoroughly. Without prompting he gave a detailed description of the events after the mutiny, what he had done himself and what he had observed.

Although this was the first interview, Hogan had already spoken with the men enough to have the general outlines of the story. He knew Joseph Thomas was under suspicion and asked Kidder about him. Did Kidder think Thomas was involved?

"I cannot say he was," Kidder replied. "He said on the passage coming here that Comstock asked him on the night of the mutiny and murders, 'Are you going into the cabin with me tonight?' To which he said, 'No, I will think of it another time.' "

Every moment of this examination was filled with peril for the six men who came back. Personal jealousy, shipboard hatred and careless observation had to be separated from facts, if possible. Hogan worked patiently.

That same day Hogan interviewed George Comstock, who might have been a key suspect, being the brother of the principal mutineer. But every man gave George a clean bill of health; the main feeling for him was sorrow because the shock of the occurrences of that midnight was so obviously still with him. Hogan seemed to sense from the beginning of his investigation that this seventeen-year-old boy was not an accomplice. In the particulars where George's observation matched Kidder's, the stories added up. George Comstock did implicate Thomas by innuendo, when he spoke of the latter's misconduct on the way to Valparaiso. Young Comstock said he was certain that Rowland Coffin was an accessory after the fact at least, and that he believed Coffin also knew of the mutiny before its commission. That charge was very serious: if proved, it would subject poor Rowland Coffin to a penalty almost as serious as that of the mutineers themselves.

Having interviewed these two, Consul Hogan mulled over his findings and turned to other business for a few days. But on June 15 he was back at the problem of the *Globe*. That day he interviewed Peter Kidder.

The Kidder brothers came to the interviews with a record of good conduct and the additional advantage that their father was a well-known ship's captain from the Vineyard. Their words, then, would carry great weight. Peter Kidder gave Thomas a bad report. He also implicated Liliston and Coffin. Liliston's guilt as an accessory was certainly obvious to all the men before the mast, but Coffin was still an unknown quantity. The Kidder report, added to George Comstock's, made it look grave for Coffin.

Consul Hogan interviewed Gilbert Smith at great length, in a friendly fashion that did not call attention to his failure to rally a group in support of the captain and the officers. Smith gave a long account of all the events after the mutiny, and he, too, cast a shadow on Joseph Thomas, Liliston and Coffin.

Another two weeks went by as Consul Hogan studied the papers before him. He conducted the last two interviews on June 30. The Hanson interview went quickly; the cook knew very little and had nothing to add to the other stories. The session with Joseph Thomas lasted much longer, Thomas sensed the importance of the hearing, and he was very careful in his answers.

Hogan asked about the causes of discontent on the voyage.

Causes? Thomas could not think of any causes for discontent. "I always had enough and the others had, as I thought, the same."

"Did the captain treat any person with violence or unnecessary severity?" Hogan knew all about the beating of Thomas on the morning of the mutiny.

"The most people had against him was his not allowing time enough to eat their victuals."

Hogan saw this was getting nowhere; Thomas was simply *not* coming out with his own animosities toward Captain Worth, so he tried another tack. "Did he flog anyone or whip him with a rope's end?"

Thomas considered. "He struck the cooper once or twice with a rope's end and he beat me with a rope's end for not coming on deck as quick as suited him when I was called."

Hogan pursued this question. "On what day did the captain beat you with a rope?"

Thomas fidgeted. "I do not recollect the day."

There it was! If Hogan had any lingering doubts about

Thomas' implication in the mutiny in some way, these were wiped out. It was incomprehensible that the man would not recall that his beating occurred on the morning before the mutiny, and was, ostensibly, the cause of the mutiny.

Hogan pressed on to get the story. "Was it not on the evening of the day when the captain and officers were killed?"

Thomas answered, again squirming, "No, it was three or four days before that."

But Thomas saw then that he must answer the questions or the presumption of his guilt would be tremendous. He opened up a little when Hogan asked him what reply Thomas had made to the captain as he threatened him with a rope's end. "I told him it would be a dear blow for him."

There was truth. It confirmed what Hogan had heard from all the others. Hogan then led Thomas through the account of the beating, which he gave honestly, and when the question of what he had done later came up, he gave the same story he had told the others aboard the *Globe*:

Q. Was there any conversation between you and Sam'l. Comstock that day?

A. He spoke a blunt word to me about the officers.

Q. What did he say to you?

A. I was aft in the evening when the sun was about half an hour high. The chief mate ordered us to go down to supper, and on passing, Samuel spoke to me and asked me if I would go down in the cabin with him tonight.

Q. What reply did you make?

A. I told him that I was sent for'd to my supper, that I would tell him by and by.

Q. Did you see any more of Comstock after supper?

A. I saw him on deck but he said nothing to me.

Michael Hogan then had all the information he could hope to get about the mutiny. He considered for a few days and consulted with others. Finally he had Joseph Thomas held in irons aboard the British man-of-war, and he released Smith,

George Comstock, the Kidder brothers, and Hanson to the freedom of the city, on their promise that they would await orders to go home and testify in any legal proceedings that would come of the *Globe* mutiny.

Hogan wrote to Secretary of State Adams on August 11, enclosing copies of the affidavits. He also sent copies to Commodore Isaac Hull, who was stationed with an American squadron at Callao. He also prepared a third set of copies, which he gave to the temporary master of the *Globe*, Captain James King, who promised to take her home and return her to her owners.

The *Globe* sailed out of Valparaiso harbor in July 1824, headed for Nantucket. Before she could arrive with her own story and her crew, the ship *Bette* pulled into the island and the tale was made known, although with many errors of fact. All this was printed in the Nantucket *Inquirer* on November 15, the day after the *Globe* actually put in at Martha's Vineyard.

The six possible mutineers were hustled off the vessel and up to Nantucket, where they were examined by Magistrate Hussey, who discharged five of the men and held Joseph Thomas over for trial in Boston.

On the day that Magistrate Hussey was holding court and examining the witnesses with the aid of the Hogan papers, the *Globe* sailed across the bar, into the harbor, and was moored at South Wharf.

Her long, desperate voyage was over.

THE
SEARCH

21

SEARCH

THE RETURN OF THE *Globe* and her story of the mutiny caused a sensation in Nantucket. Owners and ship's captains, worried frowns on their faces, called a meeting to see what could be done, for the actions of Samuel Comstock must never be allowed to be repeated aboard another whaler. If that could happen aboard the *Globe*, a notoriously easy ship in the trade, what would happen on a ship where the captain exerted real discipline with club and rope? The mutineers must be found and punished, and incidentally, their victims must be rescued and brought home safe.

There was real anguish in the Coffin family and in the rooms of the owners at the Mitchell company when the story of the mutiny was brought forth. Most upsetting was the charge that Rowland Coffin, a nephew of the owners, was deeply implicated in the mutiny, at least after the fact. Gorham Coffin, his uncle, did not believe it and set out to clear Rowland's tarnished name. He began with a letter to his congressman, Representative Reed. Soon he was writing to the new President, John Quincy Adams, to Secretary of the Navy Samuel Southard, and to many others in Washington. His dual purpose was to get a naval force moving into the Pacific to the Marshalls, discover the facts, apprehend the mutineers and save the innocent; and to clear Rowland Coffin's good name lest he be tried and hanged before he could even get home.

The other owners and captains, not vitally concerned with Rowland Coffin's case, were still personally interested in seeing that the *Globe* matter was followed through, and Washington received a good deal of mail on the subject. Secretary Southard had several letters, from Coffin, Congressman Reed and others. On January 19, 1825, he wrote Reed that he intended to send Captain Isaac Hull orders to conduct a search in the islands. He did not know how long it would be before the short-handed American navy would get the job done, but it would be done.

Southard's orders to Hull did not arrive at Callao until May. Then Hull was busy. His ships were occupied, and it was three months before anything could be done. On August 18, 1825, Lieutenant John Percival in the topsail schooner *Dolphin* was sent out to search for the suvivors of the *Globe* mutiny. Mad Jack Percival, as he was known in the squadron, was just the man for the job; he was fearless and ambitious and adventurous. It was a dull time for a navy man, what with the War of 1812 long ended, and even the Barbary pirates had been forced to become innocent traders in the Mediterranean, so the task of chasing desperate, murderous mutineers offered a bit of excitement.

Lieutenant Percival sailed from Chorillos on the coast of Peru, and so hurried was the departure in answer to Isaac Hull's orders that the ship did not have adequate provisions. The next day she stood in at Casma, a little port to the south, but could find nothing useful there, so she went on.

The cruise was leisurely. In part this was because the *Dolphin* was undertaking several tasks at once. America's navy was not such that a ship could be sent fifteen or twenty thousand miles on a single mission like the rescue of the *Globe* survivors. Lieutenant Percival was ordered to show the flag in the Pacific, call at a number of islands and secure information about them, and do any charting that came his way, for there was still a great deal of misinformation about the Pacific and there were many holes in the charts.

In September the *Dolphin* was deep in the Pacific, but far from the Marshall Islands. She visited the Caroline Islands and after that tried to make calls at a long list of atolls reported as "new" by various whaling captains. The whaler *Ganges*, out of Nantucket, had recently reported two new islands in the area, calling them Humphrey's Islands. Percival headed for the given compass points but found nothing. Had he been able to land, he would have taken possession for the United States, but he wasted a week trying to find them and came to nothing at all.

The *Dolphin* called at Duke of Clarence Island in the Kingsmills. Now they were getting warm, for the *Globe* had been here: this was the island group where chief mutineer Comstock had caused the death of that native in the canoe. As might be expected, the people of the Kingsmills had not forgotten. The excitement began almost as soon as the ship anchored. The natives came aboard, complete with shark's-tooth spears, and swaggered about the decks. They stole a few pieces of equipment and refused to give them back, no matter how threatened. They went ashore at dark, but that night the island was alive with fires and the next day canoes and sailing canoes streamed in from every direction. Soon a hundred were alongside the schooner, and although some wanted to trade, others were belligerent.

Lieutenant Hiram Paulding was officer of the watch. One islander, with shell ornaments around his neck, wrists and an-kles, insisted on coming aboard, and when the sentry raised his musket to ward him off, the native raised his spear. The sentry called for Lieutenant Paulding, who came up with a pistol loaded with bird shot; when the spearman refused to back off, Paulding shot him in the legs. The spear was dropped. The spearman became a dancer and nearly fell out of his canoe. Thereafter there was no more trouble with *him;* he remained outside the circle around the ship.

The other islanders did not go away so easily. Lieutenant Percival had been enjoined by the Secretary to explore all these islands he visited, so he attempted to go ashore here. The boat was moved in, but the moment Lieutenant Percival stepped out, he saw that he was surrounded by canoes on the outside and by armed natives making threatening gestures on the land. He ordered the men to move back to the ship, but then the people onshore tried to drag up his boat. Native divers went down to the bottom and pulled from underneath, and others threw stones at the Americans.

Several crewmen were hit, natives tried to jump over the gunwales of the boat, and one of them grabbed for a pistol. Lieutenant Percival ordered the men to open fire. They did, and one islander was severely wounded and taken into a canoe. This quieted the people down so that Lieutenant Percival could make it back to the ship.

Aboard, he tried to calm the natives. One of his pickets was moving forward, and Lieutenant Percival, to show the peaceful intentions of the Americans, took away the man's musket. He was standing talking to a native in sign language, when suddenly the native seized the musket, jumped overboard and swam mostly underwater to the shore, where in spite of musket fire directed at him, he disappeared in the bushes with his bounty.

Lieutenant Percival nearly lost his life in this affair. He was so angry with the theft of the musket that he sent boats ashore to recover it and led the first landing party himself. The boat swung in through the surf to the coral bank but caught up on the rock, and Lieutenant Percival had to wade through three feet of water to reach the shore. The boat stuck, then worked off, but the surf caught it and smashed it on the rocks so hard that every timber broke, leaving the boat's crew stranded, first in the surf and then ashore, their guns wet and useless.

Lieutenant Percival ordered the other boats away and stood there on the coral sand in full view of the hostile natives, directing fire from the ship's guns at a hut on the hill, which he supposed was some kind of headquarters. The gunfire from the ship *did* impress the islanders, and soon a small group came up, led by one man with a green branch in his hand—a sign of peace. Lieutenant Percival let him come up and then parleyed with the natives. He demanded the return of the musket. One old chief talked with others and sent a runner off. In about an hour he returned with the musket, but without either lock or bayonet. That was no good, said Lieutenant Percival. He must have the rest of it, and to emphasize the fact he ordered the ship's guns to start firing again.

Now there was a stalemate. The guns fired, the natives kept assembling and moving their war parties down to the beach. Percival led a scouting party across the island, looking for water for his ship and also to carry out the exploratory part of his mission. He was ever on the alert; he found little water, and that the island was a most unsatisfactory possession.

It was getting along to evening, and the party was in a fix. Stuck on the island, surrounded by hostile natives who might move once the sun went down, something had to be done to resolve the situation.

Two men on the ship volunteered to take a light boat ashore, and Lieutenant Paulding set them in. They managed to rescue the lieutenant and his party, but just barely. The boat nearly swamped in the surf and reached the schooner half full of water. Lieutenant Percival did not lose time in ordering the ship under way, and soon she was clear of the Kingsmills, and the dreadful legacy of the *Globe*.

The *Dolphin* stopped next at Drummond's Island, and here found extremely timorous natives who would not come aboard the vessel and trembled when the white men approached. They went ashore to fill a number of casks with water, but there were too many natives milling around; after the experience earlier, Percival changed his mind and headed on for the Marshalls.

They reached the vicinity of the Marshalls on the evening of November 19, and before dusk, sighted the most eastern islet of the chain. Now the real task would begin. Lieutenant Percival expected to have to search every one of the atolls, and even then he was not at all sure that the *Globe* mutineers had not abandoned the place and gone elsewhere.

After all, it was nearly a year since the mutiny.

22

CAPTIVE

ON THE DAY of the massacre of the men of the *Globe* at Mili, the islanders allowed William Lay and Cyrus Hussey just enough time together to assure each other that they were well-treated; then Hussey was whisked away by his protectors to another island in the atoll, and Lay wondered if they would ever meet again.

Lay's savior had been the white-haired and kindly Ludjuan, the old chief of the village above the mutineer camp, and now he took Lay to his own hut. Food was brought: breadfruit, and a fruit concoction Lay learned to call bup, and coconuts, and fish. He was offered a bath. People from the village crowded into the simple grass hut and stood or sat quietly in the background, respectful of Ludjuan and interested in his new slave.

As for Hussey, he was claimed by another chief, Lugoma, who lived in a village a considerable distance away. Lugoma was on Mili, however, for all of the people of the islands had been called to war against the white men who had established themselves on Mili and threatened their women. The high chief of all the islands, Luttuon, had called all his subchiefs together and they had brought their warriors to kill the enemy. Now it was done, and there must be a celebration before the assembled villagers broke up and went home.

THE MUTINY ON THE *GLOBE*

So Lay and Hussey did meet again, the very next day, when the islanders took both young men to the site of the tent to see the destruction. Lay and Hussey found shovels, even as their captors were wandering around among the many bits of wreckage, shouting and chanting in their glee. The boys asked their masters for permission to bury the bodies; the permission was granted, and they began the grisly work.

It was hard to match up the twisted, torn form of Silas Payne with the harsh figure of a mutineer. Even ugly little John Oliver had appeared less horrible in life than he was in death. The total abandon with which the natives had smashed the faces and heads of the victims left the two young men almost sick.

When the white boys had finished their sad duty, the islanders were growing restless. They had come to see what was to be looted and they had taken what they wanted. The casks of bread and pork and beef and other provisions had been opened, but most of the food was not to the liking of the Mili people, so it was thrown aside, scattered in the sand. The masters, however, did allow their captives to take a few belongings. Lay and Hussey both packed up a bit of flour, bread and pork. They took a blanket apiece, shoes, a few books, including Bibles, and some knives and forks.

The canoes sped off; they landed at a place near the big village Lay had visited once before, and the boys were separated. Lay cooked some pork and insisted that Hussey be brought forth to share the meal. This request seemed reasonable to their captors, so Hussey was allowed to come and eat, but the natives seemed most uneasy when the two boys spoke to each other in English, discussing the murders and their captivity.

Apparently the *Globe* had been the second or third ship these people had ever seen, for they were fascinated by everything the boys did. They giggled as Lay and Hussey used knives and forks to cut their meat. They marveled at the way they ate the cut meat. They wondered at the boys' eating and drinking at the same time, but they were not unkind; when they saw that the boys wanted water, they brought them several containers.

Before the end of this second day, Lay and Hussey began to realize that they might be saved. The islanders regarded them with the same feeling that children devote to an elephant in the zoo. Men, women and children crowded around to touch them and watch their movements. Hussey's blond hair was a sight unknown to them. They could not keep their hands away from the boys' white skin.

On the morning of February 28 the village erupted in a sea of motion. Everyone was up early, and the men began anointing themselves with coconut oil. They put on shark's-tooth necklaces, beads of coral and sea shells, and bird feathers to decorate their hair. When all was ready, the whole village moved out, with Lay and Hussey in the middle of the group, and headed for a flat piece of ground half a mile away. Here the boys discovered many more islanders, all dressed in the same finery, all stinking of coconut oil.

Then the islanders began to dance. The women of the party selected for the dance clustered behind a group of drummers. The men dancers, some three hundred of them, began to gyrate to the rhythm and the singing of the women.

Lay was blessed, or cursed, with a mighty imagination. He came to the conclusion that these were cannibals and that he was just sitting down to his own last rites. At first he believed that the dancing might be a preliminary to their entrance as *pièces de résistance,* but as it went on for hours he began to realize that it had another significance. They were being shown off as spoils, as the tale of the defeat of the evil white men was told.

For a month afterward the boys were allowed to live together in the big village. The natives treated them decently, although they watched that the whites did not try to get away. But away where? With the sailing of the *Globe* and the death of

their companions, where in the world could two lonely survivors escape to?

The boys read the Bible, but soon they discovered that the
Mili islanders objected to their reading. They did not understand the whole concept of reading—it was some kind of bad
magic to them—and they continued to be uneasy when the boys
were together speaking in English.

All went well until April. The two youths began to learn
the Marshall Islands language, and the more they became proficient, the easier their lives were. But then one day in late
March, Ludjuan informed Lay that Hussey was going to be
taken away. Lay's command of the language was not so great
that he could understand well, but it was indicated it would be
a long way away and the boys would not see each other for
many months.

Nothing was to be done. They parted then, Lay accompany-
ing the party down to the canoe landing, where Hussey and
his master, the Chief Lugoma, got into a canoe and moved
out around the point, headed for the island where Lugoma
ruled.

That day Lay ate the last of his American food, and asked
if they might not go back to the old campsite to see what
could be discovered there. His people agreed, and a half doz-
en of the natives accompanied them in a big canoe to the
place. He searched about the old tent while they caught fish in
the shallows and then they all had a feast.

The sight of the wreckage brought a pain to Lay's chest.
The tent was torn down. The charts and nautical instruments
had been torn apart and scattered, and the cases of food and
the barrels had been broken so that most of the food was rot-
ted away. Every barrel had been stove, so it was hard to find any
unspoiled meat, but Lay managed to secure some pork and a
few bits of clothing that had not been torn apart.

Then it was back to the village, and the dull life of an animal in a zoo: fed well enough by the standards of the people, treated well enough, but lonely and miserable and caged.

In April the village elders decided that there was some deadly power in Lay's book, and they destroyed his Bible. That event forced him to go outside himself; he began to seek company and made friends with an islander named Luckiair, the son-in-law of Ludjuan. Through Luckiair he obtained permission to go and to visit Hussey for a little while. They went by canoe, to arrive at Lugoma's village, and Lay and Hussey were able to spend an hour together. They were separated again, and Lay moved on to Ludjuan's son-in-law's house. After a few days Lay's protector from the Mili village came back and he was escorted home.

The months passed. Lay's clothes wore out and he was reduced to a single pair of trousers. He put these aside for bad weather, along with his only remaining shirt, and put on the belt and tassel costume of the islanders. The transition was dreadful—in a day or so his bottom was burned almost raw, and his midriff suffered almost as severely.

From time to time Hussey and Lay saw each other, but they were not in any sense allowed to become companions. Consequently both learned the ways of the islanders.

One day Lay had the feeling he was in mortal danger. The warning came from a small boy who came running up to announce to the family that the chiefs were going to kill "Wirram"—William. Lay was upset, but the family calmed him down. Then a day or so later, he heard that Hussey had been brought to the same village and that the chiefs were holding an "important meeting."

The trouble, Lay discovered, was that the islanders in some communities had come down with a new disease which involved serious swelling of the hands and feet, and even temporary blindness. The chiefs had been told that the white men had brought the disease, and they were now meeting to decide whether or not to kill the two of them. All but one of them agreed that the white men were indeed evil spirits and should be killed. Yes, said Chief Lugoma, Hussey's protector, they were evil spirits, but by destroying them, the chiefs might bring down on themselves even greater evil. The argument won the day because the vote had to be unanimous, so Lay and Hussey were saved by a narrow margin.

One summer day Lay was excited by the news that a ship had appeared on the horizon. The natives were displeased and Lay could tell they did not intend for him to leave them or for the ship to land without a fight. So he watched with mixed emotions as the ship shortened sail that afternoon and headed toward his island. All night long he hoped; then the next morning he went to the beach again, to see that the ship had disappeared.

Famine now visited the island, and Lay was reduced to a ration of half a coconut a day. Chief Ludjuan owned several coconut trees and the agile Lay climbed them at night and stole coconuts until he was suspected and had to stop. He was not caught—he had become as adept at coconut-tree climbing as any boy on the island.

So Lay's life went, a combination of exploration and bore-dom, until one morning toward the end of November 1825 when he was awakened by hooting and yelling. When he left the hut he was told that a ship had arrived at the head of the is-land. He sat and listened as the messenger consulted his chief. They were making plans to take out two war canoes, put two hundred men aboard the foreign vessel, and overpower and kill every man aboard.

23

THE FAR PLACE

CYRUS HUSSEY was never really far away from William Lay, although in the isolation imposed on the two young Americans by their captors he often felt that way. Chief Lugoma lived a day's canoe journey from Mili.

His captors did not like his European clothes, and when he protested that the sun would burn him unless he wore long shirts and pants, they said nothing; they began to destroy his clothing. But he was given much more freedom than Lay ever enjoyed. He was taught to work at repairing canoes and that became his labor. He was relatively happy, for he was treated like a son by the old chief—indeed, on several occasions, as when the crisis came in the lives of the pair with the onset of the swelling disease that struck the people, it was Hussey's foster father who interceded for them. At the second such crisis Lugoma said that if they killed the boys, they would first have to kill him. And he meant it. The others reconsidered and the boys were saved again, but it had been a narrower squeak than Lay really knew.

For reasons of personality perhaps, Hussey had a much better time of his captivity than Lay. The latter worried because he had lost his Bible. He worried because he was getting sunburned. He worried because the natives might kill him. He worried that he would never get home.

One reason for the difference in their captivity might be that Hussey was busy. Having learned to make and repair canoes, his services were in great demand. He made trips with others from one island to another to ply his trade. From time to time he came to Lay's village and they never failed to have a talk, but to Hussey, Lay always seemed upset and unhappy, which was not really his own case.

During the summer of 1825 Hussey's and Lay's people agreed that they would make a trip to some far islands, taking the white boys with them as curiosities, in the hope of securing more prestige. But when Luttuon, the head chief of the atoll, heard about this outrageous plan, he demurred. It was a great sin to even consider leaving the atoll. So the two lesser chiefs, their plan thwarted, settled down and denied they had ever thought of such a thing.

Hussey also saw much more of various sides of island life than Lay. He witnessed the murder of one islander by another. He, too, suffered through the drought, but what Lay did not know and Hussey did was that the soothsayers were again blaming the whites for the weather, suggesting that they be killed. Hussey was among the loudest advocates in his village of another view: that the drought was a judgment visited on the people because they had killed all those other whites. That view finally prevailed.

The drought was worse on Hussey's island than on Lay's. At one point his "parents" were wooking the branches of trees to make broth. At that time Hussey was so weak from hunger that he was unable to accompany his foster father on a fishing expedition.

One day at the end of the drought, a canoe came to the islands, and as was the custom, the moment the canoe reached shouting distance the paddler began yelling out his message: "War!"

High Chief Luttuon had declared war on his brother, Chief Longerene of the island they called Alloo. Hussey's father owed his allegiance to Luttuon, so he set sail that day for Mili, where Hussey and Lay were given muskets and powder and told to prepare for action. Earlier Lay had amused many of the islanders by firing a musket when asked, and by shooting off the big swivel gun which had been taken from the *Globe* and recovered at the tent site. Always, Lay's foster father had said that when they wanted to go to war they would take Lay and the swivel gun, and even if he fired only powder, it would make so much noise it would win the war.

The white boys were now considered a definite part of the society and were enlisted for the fight. They spent a day drying out powder and preparing their weapons, and the next morning started off for the island of Alloo. There were fifteen canoes in all. Landing, they headed for Longerene's village to hold the battle that would decide the power of the area. But Chief Longerene had learned of the coming of this force and had fled with his family. That was the end of the war. The islanders spent two days waiting for the chief to come back so they could kill him, but he did not return. They went home and forgot about it.

Then came November 1825, and the news that a big ship was anchored near one of the head islands.

24

THE DISCOVERY

MAD JACK Percival brought the armed schooner *Dolphin* saucily into anchorage off the easternmost of the Marshall Islands on November 19, and put the hook down in six fathoms of water a few hours later, unafraid, sitting within a cable length of the surf.

Within a matter of minutes it seemed that the islanders were upon them, surging forth in canoes, with the inevitable breadfruit and coconuts and yams. The people were friendly, they traded, and all the time the shrewd natives gathered information about their visitors.

Twenty-four hours after the Americans landed, back on Hussey's island, the excited couriers told the chief what they had seen, and Hussey sat by to interpolate. The vessel had only two masts instead of the three that the *Globe* had carried, said the messenger. What did that mean?

It meant nothing, said Hussey. The Americans had many kinds of vessels, many of them much larger than either of these.

The people had gone aboard the ships and received presents of beads, which they were wearing.

That showed the friendship of the Americans, said Hussey.

The men on board did not look like the whalers at all, said the messenger. They were stern.

Hussey recognized from the description of guns on both sides and men in uniform that they were talking about a warship, and he told them that. If the natives bothered that ship, he warned, the Americans would kill them all.

Nonsense, said the natives. They were going to take the vessel and kill all the Americans just as they had killed the whalers.

So the canoe went off to Mili, at the other end of the atoll, and the messenger brought his tale of war to High Chief Luttuon. This island was to launch its fifteen war canoes and join the fight. Hussey and his foster father Lugoma were to go, too, but their canoe was broken down again. They could not join the war party but would have to come up later.

Along came Luttuon. Hussey saw him that night in November and the high chief asked about the ship. Hussey, sensing a chance at freedom, said he believed the ship had come from America for Lay and himself. If that was true, said High Chief Luttuon, then the islanders had best kill Hussey and Lay right away so they would not tell the other Americans about the murder of Payne and the rest of the crew of the *Globe*.

That *was* a poser. Hussey thought for a moment and then offered his own answer: The people aboard the schooner knew there were two survivors, he said, and if the natives killed them, then the crew of the ship would kill all the natives. If he had achieved nothing else, Hussey had thus achieved a stalemate. The last rejoinder left the chief pulling his lip and thinking, and he went off without another word.

At the anchorage, unaware that the chiefs of the Marshalls had declared war on them, Mad Jack Percival and his men went about the tasks they saw before them in a quiet, orderly fashion. The first problem was to get water. One boat was sent ashore to explore. The men discovered two old water wells, which labor parties cleared out, and then the water gangs began to take the casks ashore. For two days they filled casks as the island messengers went off to rouse the chiefs and people for war, and while the messengers were still coming to Hussey's island, the casks were taken back aboard ship.

An exploratory party found a whaler's lance and several bits of old canvas on the island, but although Lieutenant Percival questioned dozens of islanders, not one would admit to knowing where these came from or anything about their presence.

From the behavior of the natives no one would have suspected they intended war. They came aboard the *Dolphin* in droves, wearing wreaths of flowers, shell necklaces and bracelets. They stole nothing at all and behaved with aplomb and dignity. But with the finding of the lance, the atmosphere changed subtly. Many of these natives disappeared, and Percival noticed that the largest canoes were missing, too.

After three days at anchorage, Lieutenant Percival began to look further into the atoll. Beyond, to the south and west, was a line of little islands, and that is where he would go. Their anchorage had not been very satisfactory. In an onshore wind they had to stand off and keep under weigh in order to stay out of trouble; there was not enough room for the stern to swing around in shore because the bottom dropped off so sharply here. So they moved on from that place to another island.

The next day, November 24, they stopped at one island and discovered that they had interrupted a high meeting of High Chief Luttuon and his lesser chiefs. They did not know it at the time, but the chief had William Lay concealed on that very island. After Luttuon had spoken to Hussey about killing the two white boys, the chief had not made up his mind what to do, but was planning to use the hostages as best he might in the struggle ahead.

Lieutenant Percival was no fool. He got no information from the natives, but his eyes told him much. He saw that the platforms of several of the canoes were made from the lids of sailor's chests, and it did not take him long to figure where they had come from.

The shore party at this island went inland and in one village discovered more canvas and some ash spars which had been cut into pieces. The islanders would say nothing, but Lieutenant Percival noted their intense excitement and the animated conversation that followed every one of his discoveries.

Lieutenant Percival and his party saw a village on top of the hill before them and they asked the natives what was there. Nothing, said the islanders. Just a village. All its people were here on the shore. Lieutenant Percival considered investigating but decided against it, for he had already looked over a number of huts and found nothing more than signs of some old presence.

At this moment William Lay was lying in the top rafters of one hut, concealed from the ground by the matting, with an old woman standing guard over him. She had a knife, and strict orders: if the Americans found Lay, she was to kill him then and there. The Americans were so close that Lay could hear the conversation of the men on the beach, but each time he cleared his throat, the old woman made a threatening gesture with the knife.

Lieutenant Percival's plan was to show force and hope that action would push the natives into revealing whatever they knew about the mutiny. Not knowing that the islanders had murdered nearly all the survivors, there is no way he could have known that Luttuon did not dare admit the truth or anything about the affair. For Cyrus Hussey's argument about certain retaliation if they were harmed was convincing; Luttuon was not high chief without knowing the ways of men, and he now had to extricate the islanders from a difficult situation. The two white boys were among his most important weapons.

All afternoon the American navy men searched around this village but found nothing more to link the place to the *Globe*.

They had not even done that, really, but had only established the fact that whalers had been here. The sea chests were the most telling evidence that the whalers had been more than a landing party.

Toward sundown it was a stand-off between the islanders and the sailors. Lieutenant Percival called his men aboard for the night, and the *Dolphin* stood out to sea to avoid the sharp coral reef. The natives then got into their canoes and went off across the lagoon.

By this time Percival had a good idea of the geography of the atoll. It consisted of a large number of islets lying in a circle around the blue lagoon, like a bracelet around a lady's arm. Some of the islands were connected at low tide by coral reef. Others had to be reached by canoe. Apparently the atoll was the rim of a huge volcano whose center had blown out millions of years ago, and which had sunk into the sea until only the little tops showed in the circle.

If the *Dolphin* could negotiate the entrance through the reef, it would be much simpler to take her in and search from within the perimeter, rather than have to stand off and on the shore because of the deep water that jutted right up to the beach and left no anchorage. So the next morning, November 25, Lieutenant Percival ordered the ship to try to go in. He anchored in nine fathoms of water, just off the entrance to the lagoon, and then, working his light sails so there would not be too much strain, he attempted to cross. But the reef was just too high, and the *Dolphin* drew too much to cross it.

That failure worried Lieutenant Percival because it made his operation almost ineffectual. He had to send out shore parties, several of them, if he was to accomplish his mission. But with two or three boats gone, he did not have enough men to work the ship properly, and she was hard to manage in this water with its deeps and shallows, reefs and treacherous currents, caused by the lagoons and tides. Still, something must be done. Lieutenant Percival ordered Paulding to send eleven men and a boat through the passage into the lagoon, then canvass the islands for signs of the men of the *Globe*. The boat would stand offshore inside the lagoon and serve as transport and lookout for the armed force.

They were not going to get any help from the natives, Percival sensed that. So they had to be unusually vigilant to discover the truth.

The party went ashore, and by evening had gotten out of sight.

The next morning dawned bright and clear, and Lieutenant Paulding went out in the boat to find his landing party and see what they had discovered. The party had traversed several islands, and had not been bothered by the natives. Instead, the sailors had been offered coconuts and other food without any request for payment. More important, they had found a mitten with the name "Rowland Coffin" on it.

That name meant nothing to the landing party, but to Paulding, who had a crew list of the *Globe* in hand—there it was, sticking out like a sore thumb. The *Globe* had been here! That was all the Americans found that day.

The next day, November 26, was cold and squally and Paulding stayed with the boat while the landing party scoured the shore and the wooded inland. The ship's surgeon was with them on this excursion, and although he had been ill for some time since sailing from Peru, it was a shock this day when he died suddenly. The Americans held a burial ceremony then, an occasion indicative of some of the cultural problems between the sailors and the natives: the sailors assembled in full-dress uniform on the shore to pay their respects to the surgeon. The grave was dug, the body lowered, the services read. The islanders stood behind the knot of men watching silently. Then the guard of honor fired the musket salute in the air, and the natives erupted in bursts of laughter and shouting. Furious, the Americans drove the natives away from the grave site. This disrespect was as maddening to them as it had been the day before to the natives when Paulding, with nothing better to do, had shot down a number of the islanders' pet herons, just for target practice.

By this time the suspicion was strong on both sides. Luttuon was sure the Americans, with their fearsome vessel, were set upon exterminating his people, and if possible he intended to seize that vessel and kill *all* the foreigners. Lieutenant Percival felt the islanders were hiding something, men or a secret, and he determined to discover what it was. Neither side was inclined to meet on even terms with the other. The suspicions were growing, not diminishing.

On November 27 the search party continued to move northward and westward along the island chain. Percival intended to search each atoll until he found his answers. Crossing a long reef, the sailors came to an islet connected with a large island. There they saw the big village to which Lay and Hussey had first been taken, and where Lay had lived until spirited into the jungle on Luttuon's orders.

Lieutenant Paulding was leading the expedition this morning. The men marched across the sandy beach. Suddenly, at the extreme east end of the islet, Paulding spotted some pieces of flotsam, and on coming upon them, saw that they were staves of barrels, and bits of old canvas and clothing. Farther on they stopped and started digging. They found a skeleton, although they did not know whose it was. They found a box containing a few Spanish dollars.

Looking around for the natives who trailed them all the time, Paulding saw that they had all disappeared into the jungle as the white men went to the old tent site, for that is where they were. Obviously there was something important here. At a swift pace Lieutenant Paulding led his men up the beach, but found nothing more. As darkness closed down on them they took possession of an unoccupied hut and bedded down for the night, spotting a watch and building a fire.

During the night the islander runners reached Luttuon's

camp and informed him that the Americans had found the place where all the white men were killed and had discovered at least one body. Luttuon now determined to force the issue. Tomorrow, he said, he would fight the white men, beat them, and then take the canoes and seize their ship. He called for Lay to be brought to him and began asking questions, with considerable acumen. Lay was now spirited to a new hiding place, and the war drums began to beat.

Hussey had been held at Luttuon's headquarters for several days. Every day the chief called him to ask questions about the Americans and the ship. Since Hussey had not seen the ship, although Lay had seen it, Hussey was not very informative. So Luttuon called in the medicine man, who began knotting up leaves—his way of preparing to predict the future.

The whole island was agitated. People moved to and fro recounting their adventures with the white men, and particularly noting that there was always one question: What happened to the white men who were here before? That, of course, was the question no one on the island would ever answer for a stranger.

But the Americans suspected that some strange tragedy lay before them. They also expected trouble. It came on the morning of November 29, when they set out on their line of march and almost immediately discovered the natives lined before them in battle formation.

The sailors decided to retreat. But when they got back to the hut where they had spent the night—a fine defensive position—the hut was gone. They had found a canoe earlier and had kept that at the hut site. The canoe was gone. Their guns were wet from the rain, and their ammunition was soaked. If they had to fight, it would have to be with cutlass and bayonet.

The officer in charge of the party stopped and sent two men to the schooner to bring help. The messenger found the ship at noon and reported to Lieutenant Percival. Noting that the natives had many opportunities in the past week to make trouble but had not, Percival came to the conclusion that the mutineers were among the natives and had excited them to attack. At four o'clock in the afternoon he sent a very heavily armed party out to the aid of the search group. Lieutenant Paulding was in charge, another officer was with him, plus fourteen men. The expedition left the ship badly depleted in crew, but Percival was willing to take the risk.

Paulding took the heavy boat in over the reef and moved up the lagoon. He arrived at the camp at eight o'clock in the evening, worried that the natives had already attacked, but he found the men all safe and no natives nearby.

The next morning the large American party set out and was confronted soon enough by a huge assemblage of islanders near a big village. When Paulding decided that he would go up and search those huts, and began to move, Luttuon ordered the women and children sent back to the village so they would not be hurt in the impending fighting.

Both sides were ready for battle, but the natives so outnumbered the Americans that the issue was very much in doubt. Still, Paulding had no recourse. He had been sent to do a job, and he and his men were ready. They loaded their guns and prepared for what might come. The boat came in to shore, dropped anchor, and headed into the surf.

Just as the sailors were ready to leap out of the boat, a figure stepped forward and spoke to them, in English.

25

THE RESCUE

WILLIAM LAY had been trying to persuade Luttuon and his chiefs that he could be of assistance in the coming fight against the white men. Luttuon, no fool, consulted the gods, and they were undecided. The gods were worried that these people were of Lay's land and that he would instruct them in how to murder the islanders.

Lay informed Luttuon that his country had no ships with two masts. Luttuon knew that was a lie because Hussey had already told him that all countries in his part of the world had ships with various numbers of masts. But Luttuon still listened.

The gods were consulted several times, and finally they agreed that the young white man should be allowed to accompany the war party as it went to seize the ship. Luttuon set out with two units, one a sea party of two huge canoes, each bearing fifty warriors, which would take the ship. The rest of the warriors advanced by land to assault the landing party that was known to be coming to the islands. So on the morning of November 29 Luttuon and his party were lying in wait for the boat to land, shouting and gesticulating, waving spears, building their courage and fighting spirit as they always did. William Lay went to Luttuon and said he would fight the boat's crew. But first he would go down and talk to these other white men. He would decieve them and persuade them to come on-shore and sit down, and stack their arms nearby. Then Luttuon and his warriors, silent as the shark, would swoop down upon the white men, seize their fearsome muskets and pistols, and kill them all.

"Ha!" one chief shouted. "He will go down and help them. The white men will stick together."

But Luttuon listened. Then he called the medicine man, and the two of them retired to ask the gods what they thought of the idea. He returned to tell the other chiefs that the gods thought the young white's plan was excellent and that they should follow it.

At this time Lieutenant Paulding's boat was less than a hundred yards offshore, heading in purposefully, and the island-ers could see the sailors with their muskets and bayonets.

Luttuon called Lay. He oiled the boy's head and body with sacred coconut oil and told him to do as he had promised he would. Then William Lay set out for the beach, accompanied by a hundred warriors. He warned them sternly that they were to make no show of force or unfriendliness until he said the word. Fifty yards from the shore Lay made the warriors sit down and put their weapons beside them. Then he walked on, and spoke to the American officer.

At the edge of the surf Lieutenant Paulding stared at this strange-looking native who spoke to him in English. The man's hair was long, combed up and tied in a knot on top of his head. Around his loins he wore the island costume. His skin was al-most black, and the coconut oil made it shine. This "native" addressed Lieutenant Paulding again.

"Don't come on shore unless you are prepared to fight," he said. "The islanders are going to kill you."

Paulding continued to stare. He knew this must be one of the men they had come to get, but it seemed impossible that he was anything but a native. Then a second thought entered his mind. This must be one of the mutineers—otherwise would he not come flying down to the beach?

"What is your name?" he asked.

"William Lay."

"Were you a member of the crew of the ship *Globe*?"

"Yes, I was."

Paulding consulted his papers. The look of the young man, if one could penetrate beneath the surface, was proper for William Lay. He seemed the right age—shipped at seventeen would make him nineteen years old.

"Come to the boat," Paulding told Lay.

"I don't dare. If I do, the natives will attack."

"Run! We will protect you."

"The people will kill me before I can get there."

All this occurred while the islanders behind Lay were calling to him and asking him how he progressed in his plan to lure the Americans ashore so they could be stoned to death.

"Wait," he said. "A little more time."

Lieutenant Paulding took the initiative. "Discharge your weapons," he cried to his men. The sound of shots rang raggedly through the air.

"Reload."

Each man reloaded his weapon, making sure it was dry and ready.

"Now, onto the beach."

They moved off the boat then, through the surf, weapons high to keep them dry, and marched up to where Lay was standing. Paulding took out his revolver and pointed it straight at Lay's breast. He knew he risked frightening the boy into panic, but he could see no other way to take him without provoking the islanders to another murder. "Who are you?" he asked loudly and fiercely.

"I am your man," said Lay and broke down, weeping.

Paulding then told Lay to tell the natives they must not rise from where they were sitting or throw any stones. "We will shoot them all if they do," he added. He looked around him. Each man carried a pistol and a full cartridge box.

Lay was quite overcome at having heard the voice of a strange white man for the first time in a year and a half. He tried to speak to the islanders, but broke down in a gibberish of half English, half island language. "They are going to kill me, they are going to kill me!" he cried.

Paulding grabbed him by the arm. "Why did you say we are going to kill you?" he demanded.

"I'm sorry," Lay replied. "I was so overcome, I didn't know what I was saying."

Lieutenant Paulding now pointed ashore. The natives were getting up. They appeared very restless, and two or three began to advance. Paulding pointed his gun at one and swung it meaningfully in a wide arc.

"Tell them that we shall shoot them all if they come any further," he said to Lay, and Lay translated the warning.

The islanders stopped, all but one old man—Lay's foster father. He was unarmed, and his hair was white. He came forward slowly.

"Don't hurt him," Lay said. "This is Ludjuan, my protector."

The old man came up and took Lay's hand in both of his.

"What are these people going to do with you, my son?" he asked.

"Don't worry," Lay said. He embraced the old man tenderly and said he would see him again before he left the island. Then he wept again.

Lieutenant Paulding was growing nervous under the watchful eyes of the islanders who stood up above, their spears and stones in hand, but apparently with no intention of attacking. Still the odds were ten to one, and who knew how many natives lurked back there beyond the palm line? He cut short the discussion between Lay and his foster father and hurried Lay down to the boat, the guard behind him.

Lay broke down completely on the thwarts. A babble of questions came from his lips. How were all the people in East Saybrook? he asked. Then he remembered that these rescuers would not know anyone in East Saybrook, Connecticut, unless by chance. He kept asking questions about home but paid no attention to the answers, repeating himself time after time.

Lieutenant Paulding waited a little while and then began interrogating Lay about the *Globe*. What had happened to the crew that was left behind?

"They are all dead except Cyrus Hussey," Lay said gravely, "and he is over there." He pointed to an island a few miles to windward.

Lay then told Lieutenant Paulding all that he knew about the ship and its crew, and how Chief Luttuon had sent spies to the ship every day as gawkers and traders, and how shrewdly they had appraised the vessel and its force of men and guns. Paulding was impressed by the minute knowledge that the islanders had gained of their movements and strength. Lay told him that the islanders had been ready to attack a number of times, but that he and Hussey had so far stopped them, by such wild talk as that the ship's cannon could sink an island. He told of one plan that had been advanced in the councils of the island: to bore a hole in the bottom of the *Dolphin* with an auger they had rescued from the *Globe* tool chest, to watch the ship sink, and then massacre the whites as they came ashore. This was hardly felicitous information to be giving Lieutenant Paulding, who was on his way to the other island to rescue Hussey.

As they headed out, it was growing late in the day, and the strains of Lay's rescue were telling on the ship's boat crew. Lieutenant Paulding landed on a dry reef about halfway to the island, to give the men a break. Lay was very nervous all the time they remained. He had visions of Luttuon's anger: he could see the chief sending off a messenger to Lugoma demanding that he kill Hussey before the Americans could capture him.

Had he not threatened to do just that a dozen times? Or if the chiefs did not kill his friend, they might spirit him away to some other island group.

Lieutenant Paulding heard Lay's complaint, and as soon as the men had eaten some biscuits and field rations, he set out again, and landed on Lugoma's island. No one saw them coming and they were almost on the beach before they were observed. Lugoma and several other people came down to the beach; they saw Lay in his native costume still, and called out to him, "Wirrum, what are you doing here and what do you want?"

Lay replied, but before Lugoma could get close enough to hear, Paulding leaped from the boat, grasped Lugoma by the shoulder and pointed his pistol at him. Looking at Lay, he said, "Tell him that unless Hussey is brought here immediately, I shall kill him."

Lugoma pleaded for mercy. "Don't kill me," he said. "He is here and I will send for him." He spoke to one of the women with him. She ran off, and a few moments later returned with Hussey.

Cyrus Hussey's appearance was even more impressive than Lay's: dressed like Lay in the native costume, with a piece of blanket about his loins, and his body black from the sun, his long yellow hair streamed down in ringlets.

As Hussey approached, Lieutenant Paulding asked him, "Well, young man, do you wish to return to your country?"

Hussey's eyes filled with tears at the prospect, as Lay's had before him.

"Yes, sir," he replied. "I know of nothing that I have done for which I should be afraid to go home."

26

THE END
OF THE GLOBE

ALTHOUGH THE BOYS had lived as slaves in this island chain for nearly two years, the partings were sad affairs, particularly between Hussey and Lugoma, for the boy and the chief had become quite attached to each other over the many months. Lugoma made Hussey promise to come back to them, and made Lieutenant Paulding promise to bring him back. Paulding evaded the issue by saying he would let Hussey return if his mother was agreeable. Lugoma pondered that remark and then agreed that that was the way it should be.

Lay and Hussey were taken aboard the schooner and treated to baths, shaves and haircuts. Their hair had been growing for twenty-two months without a cutting, and as the blond locks of Hussey fell to the deck they were as luxurious as those of any young girl.

The part of the boys now was to enjoy themselves and the feeling of going home. But there was one more official task for Lieutenant Percival to perform here in the islands, and he needed the help of Lay and Hussey as interpreters. Dressed in his best uniform, with his weapons, Percival took a shore party to the island and informed the natives through Lay and Hussey that he demanded a meeting with the chiefs in council. He had something important to discuss.

The chiefs and most of the warriors were still on Alloo Island, where they were not quite sure what they were going to do. Lieutenant Percival sent insistent messages, but he also gave many gifts, including some to Ludjuan, the "father" of William Lay, and the lieutenant made sure Ludjuan was informed that these were rewards for saving the young man's life.

The islanders stalled for several days. On December 2 Lieutenant Percival tired of it—he was never a man of long patience —and he let the natives know that if the chiefs did not arrive at the meeting place before sunset, he would go ashore with fifty men and many guns and kill everyone he saw. This threat, which Percival had no intention of carrying out, had precisely the desired effect. The islanders were thrown into consternation, messengers were sent to Alloo immediately, the chiefs paddled furiously across the lagoon, and Percival went back to the ship to dine and wait. After dinner Lay and Lieutenant Paulding went ashore on a bird-shooting expedition, and while they were gone the word came that the chiefs would meet with the lieutenant and his officers the next morning.

That morning Hussey, Lay and Lieutenant Percival went ashore bearing many gifts for the chiefs, and they met them in a big hut on top of the hill. The lieutenant began by telling them he had been sent by the head chief of his country to look for the men of the *Globe,* only to find that all but two had been murdered. This was a very serious offense against his chief. Since it was the first time, Percival said, it could be forgiven, but if the islanders should ever again kill or injure a white man who came there, the great chief would send a naval force and exterminate everything on the island, from the palm trees to the people.

Having spoken with such authority, Lieutenant Percival then instructed Lay to present the gifts. There were three decorative tomahawks, an ax, a bag of beads, a number of cotton handkerchiefs, two hogs, several cats. These were all handed

194

over, plus potatoes and corn, along with pumpkin and other seeds.

That was the end of the meeting. The Americans went back to the ship. Later in the day Lieutenant Percival, like the good naval officer he was, took a boat around the island to make a topographical survey, and then the ship anchored for the night.

On December 4 the ship sailed to the point where the *Globe* had lain, and anchored. A landing party went ashore and dug up the skull, bones and cutlass of Samuel Comstock from the grave where he was buried. They took the skull and cutlass for delivery home and reburied the rest.

For the next three days Lieutenant Percival remained in the islands, making friends with Luttuon and his chiefs, planting seeds and assuring the people of the friendship of the Americans. Meanwhile his ship's boats completed the surveys of the island group for the naval chart makers.

On December 7 they sailed away from the Marshalls, looking for other islands in the area that had been reported by whaling captains. They stopped once at South Pedder's Island, a few miles away from Mili, and then sailed for the Hawaiian Islands, reaching Oahu on January 14.

There the men of the *Dolphin* got into a scrape involving Captain Worth's friend, the Reverend Mr. Bingham. That religious gentleman had tired of the whalers and their habits; such men as Lewis, Prass and the other four ship-jumpers from the *Globe* had stirred up the natives, drunk quantities of rum and gin, wreaked havoc with the female population, brought tuberculosis and syphilis to the natives, and immorality to boot. Mr. Bingham persuaded the royal house of Hawaii to lower a *tabu* on the women of Honolulu when the *Dolphin* sailed in with her crew of American hearties, and the sailors were so infuriated that they went out and tried to burn down Mr. Bingham's house. They were restrained by the Hawaiian soldiers when they also attacked the house of a chief, and the whole disgraceful affair created a serious animosity between American sailors and the people of the islands.

The two young survivors had to wait while Lieutenant Percival conducted his other business. The ship did not sail from Oahu until May 11.

In mid-July the *Dolphin* reached Valparaiso, where the name of the *Globe* was well known. A few days of shore leave, a transfer to the frigate *United States* at Callao, and then a journey back to Valparaiso, where the two survivors were moved to the *Brandywine*. They finally reached New York on April 22, 1827. They had been away from home for nearly five years.

In Nantucket they found a changed whaling industry, for the mutiny aboard the *Globe* had caused whaling men and the American government to take a new look at the ships and men who sailed in search of oil. The *Dolphin's* cruise was to show the flag and give protection to Americans on the high seas as much as to rescue the two *Globe* survivors and solve the mystery of the others. More important to sailing men, the owners of Nantucket changed the status of the harpooners, or boatsteerers. No longer did they live in that half-world between forecastle and cabin, but were now treated as pure specialists. They stood no watches and they had nothing to do with the running of the ship.

These changes were great, but when Lay and Hussey came home to Nantucket they found the whaling industry prosperous, the wharves were packed with whalers coming and going, and the town was filled with sailors waiting for their ships.

Lay and Hussey also found that their old companions' lives had changed a great deal. Gilbert Smith had been shown great compassion by the owners, who gave him the post of "master" of the *Globe*. But he never sailed in her. He went out as a mate in another whaler, and then as a captain, and finally settled in France when entrepreneurs in that land decided they wanted to establish their own whaling fleet.

Anthony Hanson, one of the beachcombers shipped at

Oahu, simply disappeared from Nantucket after all the excitement was over. No one ever discovered what happened to him.

Peter Kidder went back to sea on a whaler and was drowned in 1827 when his whaleboat capsized during a furious chase.

Stephen Kidder sailed once more on the *Globe* and after a long career at sea, settled down in Martha's Vineyard, where he died in 1871.

Joseph Thomas stood trial in Boston for his alleged part in the mutiny, but by the time the trial was held, people had lost interest in the case, the witnesses were scattered, and no one could prove to a jury that he had actually known about the mutiny long enough before it was committed to do anything to save the captain or the other officers. He was acquitted and immediately dropped out of sight.

George Comstock quickly disappeared as well. He never recovered from the shock of seeing his brother coming out of the cabin that dreadful night, all bloody and full of fury. He forsook whaling and the sea, and ended up in San Francisco. Another brother, William Comstock, later corresponded with George and wrote a biography of Samuel Comstock, to help people understand that strange, twisted character.

William Lay and Cyrus Hussey were popularly cleared of all connection with the mutiny. When Commodore Hull declared them to be of good character, a federal judge released them from the naval service they had been in since working their way home on the *Dolphin*. Later they collaborated on a book about their experiences. They seem to have had the good will of George Comstock in this venture, for there are many quotations from a brief narrative of the mutiny that George wrote, perhaps at their request, since he was the closest thing to an eyewitness. Lay then dropped out of sight, and apparently did not go back to sea. Cyrus Hussey went to sea again, in the tradition of the Husseys of Nantucket, on the ship *Congress*. But those months of famine on Mili had taken their toll, for he never made it back to the island to visit Lu-goma; he died on his whaling voyage as the *Congress* rounded Cape Horn.

As for the ship herself, she was refurbished and put back in condition, and went out again as a whaler, under Captain Reuben Swain II. In fact, she was already gone again on an-other greasy voyage when Lay and Hussey came home. The *Globe* returned in May 1828, with a respectable 2,105 barrels of oil aboard. Then she was sold to Captain George Macy for $5,000, and he took her into the South American trade. She grew old and tired and was finally broken up in South Ameri-ca, to remain no more than a legend in the history of Nan-tucket and American whaling.

As for Samuel Comstock, his name went down in the histo-ry of infamy, and only his father, that quiet Quaker from New York, was left to say a word for him. When the *Globe* arrived back in Nantucket after the mutiny, and the terrible story was revealed in all its gory detail, the heartsick Nathan Comstock had but one comment to make. Shaking his head and nearly weeping, he said it:

"Oh, Samuel, poor heaven-forsaken Samuel."

BIBLIO-GRAPHICAL NOTE

SOME YEARS AGO, while reading Edouard Stackpole's *The Sea Hunters* and being fascinated by his capsule account of the mutiny aboard the whaler *Globe*, I felt that this story should really be told in all its detail. That was the genesis of the book. Mr. Stackpole, Mrs. Louise Hussey and William Walmsley of the Foulger and Whaling museums in Nantucket were all extremely helpful to me in casting this book. They made available manuscripts and other material to me that were vital to the work, and I am grateful to them all.

One reason the *Globe* story lends itself so well to modern telling is the abundance of detail of the mutiny and the voyage as well as the adventures of the various members of the crew. This is because so many of them told their stories after the famous mutiny was all over. William Lay and Cyrus Hussey told their story of mutiny and captivity in *A Narrative of the Mutiny on Board the Whaleship Globe,* published by subscription in 1828 in New London, Connecticut. The subtitle is: *And the Journal of a Residence of Two Years on the Mulgrave Islands, with Observations on the Manners and Customs of the Inhabitants.*

Then there is William Comstock's book *The Terrible Mutineer,* a biography of Samuel Comstock, the leader of the uprising. William was Samuel's brother, a whaling man himself, who was at sea on another ship at the time of the mutiny. His book is based on personal knowledge, letters home from Samuel, and conversations and material from George Comstock, who was there. George Comstock also wrote his own version, a *Narrative of the Mutiny, Capture and Transactions on Board the Ship Globe of Nantucket,* an unpublished manuscript in the Nantucket Whaling Museum.

The National Archives has on deposit the records of U.S. Consul Michael Hogan at Valparaiso, in its general records of the Department of State. These consular dispatches include statements made when the *Globe* was returned by six of its crew members to Valparaiso in 1824. The crew members were Gilbert Smith, Peter and Stephen Kidder, George Comstock, Anthony Hanson (the ship's cook) and Joseph Thomas, a suspected mutineer and known beachcomber who had shipped on the *Globe* at Hawaii shortly before the mutiny. These affidavits give invaluable details of the mutiny and the aftermath.

The log of the schooner *Dolphin* is also in the National Archives. Correspondence between Gorham Coffin and various figures is in the hands of the Whaling Museum at Nantucket.

The U.S. Navy sent Lieutenant John Percival and the schooner *Dolphin* to the South Seas to find the mutineers and their victims. After that remarkable journey, which included calls at most of the newly discovered savage islands where whalers might or might not be mistreated by natives, Paulding wrote a book about it. It was published in 1831 by G. and C. and H. Carvill of New York. I used the copy in the Whaling Museum.

Edouard Stackpole very kindly lent me a copy of his juvenile novel *Mutiny at Midnight,* which was published in 1939, and which was very helpful for setting the scene for a book on whaling.

I have taken no more than slight artistic license with the

language. There was one vacancy in the research material—any account among the survivors of the actual processes of whaling. They were writing for an informed audience and their subject was the dreadful mutiny and its aftermath. They can be forgiven for believing that everyone knew the scene, and the subject of whaling. I borrowed from William B. Davis' *Nimrod of the Sea* and J. Ross Browne's *Etchings of a Whaling Cruise* for the whaling material. I also used materials from the extensive clipping file of the Whaling Museum, which was brought to my attention by its librarian, Mrs. Hussey.

About the Author

EDWIN P. HOYT has been writing books on naval affairs and the sea for some fifteen years. Before that time he was a newspaper reporter and editor, magazine editor, television producer, and sometime sailor. He is married and has three grown children. His wife is also a writer, and artist. They live now on Nantucket Island, off the coast of Massachusetts.

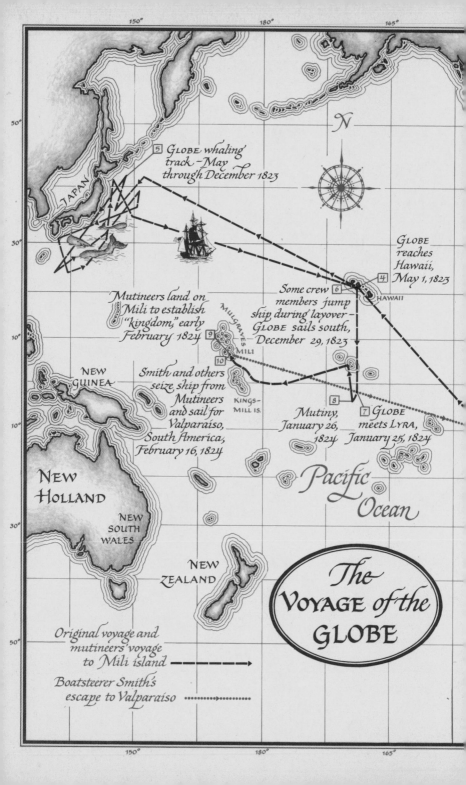

The Voyage of the
GLOBE

5 GLOBE whaling
track – May
through December 1823

GLOBE
reaches
Hawaii,
May 1, 1823

4

Some crew
members jump
ship during layover –
GLOBE sails south,
December 29, 1823

6

HAWAII

Mutineers land on
Mili to establish
"kingdom," early
February 1824

9

MULGRAVES

10 MILI

Smith and others
seize ship from
Mutineers
and sail for
Valparaiso,
South America,
February 16, 1824

KINGS-
MILL IS.

Mutiny,
January 26,
1824

8

7 GLOBE
meets LYRA,
January 25, 1824

Pacific
Ocean

NEW
GUINEA

NEW
HOLLAND

NEW
SOUTH
WALES

NEW
ZEALAND

JAPAN

Original voyage and
mutineers' voyage
to Mili island

Boatsteerer Smith's
escape to Valparaiso